# The Graffiti I Didn't Do, The Prison Time I Did

*A Memoir*

Betty Baer

Epigraph Books
Rhinebeck, New York

Book design by Colin Rolfe
Cover photo © Rocky Kneten Photography

Library of Congress Control Number: 2016936311

ISBN: 978-1-944037-22-2

Printed in the United States of America

Epigraph Books
22 East Market Street, Suite 304
Rhinebeck, New York 12572
(845) 876-4861
www.epigraphps.com

For my sons.

# Part I

# Chapter 1
# What Really Happened

**April, 28th, 1981.**

At three in the morning, the air was still and humid. The few skyscrapers that make up downtown Houston were deserted. A Volkswagen Rabbit slowly approached Bell Street. Tom parked the car in the shadows of the streetlight's ambient glow. Maria, fresh-faced and petite, hopped out of the passenger side of the car. Tom exited the driver's side, reaching for the cans of red spray paint in the back seat. The Exxon building lay ahead of them. They sprinted through the immaculate lawn and up to the massive entrance facade. Once called the Humble Oil building, it was the first skyscraper in Texas and held its place as a beacon to the energy industry.

Tom snapped off the paint cylinder cap as he approached the marble wall surrounding the building. He raised his arm and wrote, "Red, White, and Blue." Maria finished with, "We spit on you. May Day, 1981."

They charged back to the unlocked car. Maria jumped in and closed the door behind her while Tom grazed his head getting into the driver's seat. As he fastened his seatbelt and turned the ignition key, screeching brakes shattered the silence. A taxicab appeared at the corner of the cross street.

"Shit," Tom said.

"Do you think he saw us?" Maria asked.

Tom squinted. The cab driver, a round, gray form, hobbled out of his cab and up to the Exxon building. Tom's foot gingerly pressed the gas pedal as he navigated the car away from the building and the cab driver.

"I don't know if he saw us, but he had to see the spray painting," Tom said.

Tom drove down side streets, checking his rearview mirror until they reached Houston's East End. After dropping off Maria at her second-floor garage apartment, Tom took I-45 to the Gulfgate exit and returned home. He parked the car in the driveway and walked up the two cracked concrete steps to the house on Bradford Street. Not wanting to wake the kids, he gently unlocked the front door and soundlessly walked into the house, making his way in the dark past the multilevel gerbil cage taking up most of the living room and into the bedroom. He removed his clothes and climbed into bed.

"Close call," he sighed. "I hope that cab driver didn't see us."

I rolled over. Did Tom mumble something about a cab driver? I wiggled the blanket off my shoulders and placed it over him. His warm body close to mine was all I needed to drift back to sleep. Tom was safely home. Mission accomplished.

### Three days later.

Here it was, May 1st, 1981, and we were still at it. The Revolutionary Communist Party, known as the RCP, organized a noon rally to celebrate May Day in downtown Houston. Or rather they were still at it and I was following along because, although I recently departed the RCP, I didn't know what else to do.

I was a baby boomer coming of age in the late 1960s. Growing up and going to college in New York, I was radicalized like so many of my peers. I marched in Anti-Vietnam War protests; venerated the Black Panthers; toasted Che Guevara; blissed out to the Grateful Dead. No longer the sheltered suburban teen who equated politics with voting, I chanted support for wars of liberation from South East Asia to Angola to Bolivia. These were places I wouldn't have found on a map in high school.

Suddenly what happened in the world mattered. My respect for democracy in the U.S. crumbled as I learned about my government propping up dictators in Chile and Iran. Corporate profit-making turned sinister when I understood money-making in Apartheid South Africa was business as usual.

Eighteen-year-old teenage boys were considered old enough to be drafted but had to wait until they were twenty-one to vote. The hypocrisy I never noticed was the subject of daily discussion. I questioned authority, when at one time I didn't realize there was an authority to question. A whole new perspective and possibility of change opened up to me. It was a unique time in American history, when middle-class youth joined with those fighting for civil rights, women's rights, and a nation's right to self-determination. It was the most liberating feeling I ever experienced.

As the radical movements of the 1960s and '70s retracted and most of the young activists folded back into their prescribed life path, I took my commitment to another level and joined the RCP. As thrilling as the '60s were and significant as the gains made, I knew we did not come close to creating a just society. That would take a change in the whole system of government. That would take a revolution.

Why? Because Marxism, Leninism, and Chairman Mao  told us so. We believed their method of economic analysis was as true as the science that says the earth revolves around the sun. We had no doubt that embracing their teachings would lead to a future altruistic society. This all-encompassing certainty gave my life purpose. It gave me a community of comrades that was as close as family. It gave me no other way to see how humans relate to the world or themselves.

At some point, as much as I recognized the inequalities of capitalism, I questioned the certainty of its doom. If doomed it was, I questioned whether Marx, Lenin and Mao had come up with a viable alternative. I couldn't ignore my country's claim of totalitarian dictatorship in communist countries as all bourgeois propaganda. I was beginning to think that clamping down on opposition never works in the long term regardless of the system of government.

Even if the violent part of revolution was far-off in the future, I was wondering if violence did only breed violence. If I could embrace a utopia of equality for all, then why settle for one that included violence to get there? I still thought it was possible to make the world a better place, but I was paralyzed by questions. For so many years, I had had answers. Now this was a void I couldn't fill. Tom had his doubts as well. The spray painting was a kind of farewell act for him as he left the party, too.

There was a part of me that still yearned to embrace something larger than myself, to be part of something meaningful. Partly out of habit and a large part not wanting my comrades to think I was a total sellout, I joined the others on Capitol Street for the May Day rally. It was, after all, International Workers Day and was celebrated in many parts of the world. It wasn't some cult-like idea the RCP cooked up. The theme of May Day, 1981, was nuclear disarmament. I could unite with that.

\* \* \*

A small group of protesters congregated beneath a banner, which read, "Stop the American and Soviet Nuclear Arms Buildup!" Within minutes after the rally started, a handful of uniformed police arrived. They perched on the corner, surveying our every movement. I looked both ways before stepping off the curb, reaching out and handing a May Day flyer to a passerby.

This May Day rally, the police didn't hesitate to go into action. They swooped down for arrests after the first flyers left our hands. When the rest of the country saw the end of protests in the late 1970s, Houston proved different. The police murder of Joe Campos Torres in 1975 lit a fire of outrage in Houston, especially in the Hispanic community. Ever since, activists were targeted by the police. Participating in a protest, no matter how small and uneventful, could lead to arrest. Littering, obstructing a passageway, and disorderly conduct were the "charges" for passing out flyers and holding up protest signs. I knew this and had been arrested several times in this manner.

Participating in May Day would surely show that I didn't leave the RCP because I was a coward.

One after the other, people were rounded up and led away. The street was cleared of demonstrators before the demonstration even began. I was noticeably spared. Police walked right by me as if I wasn't there. Did they know that I was not an RCP threat anymore? It was creepy. Something was going on.

I heard footsteps coming from behind me. I turned around and spotted Morris Quast, a plainclothes police officer from the Criminal Intelligence Division (CID) of the Houston Police.

"Miss Sullivan?" he asked.

"Yes," I said as if he was asking for directions.

"Morris Quast," he said, flipping open his suit jacket to display his badge.

His dark glasses and formal manner didn't hide the fact that he knew my name and I his. I would recognize his straggly salt and pepper hair and six foot boxy frame anywhere.

"You are charged with criminal mischief for spray painting the Exxon building on April 28, 1981."

This didn't make sense. I didn't know how to react. My first instinct was to say, "What are you talking about?" Getting arrested at a rally was all-too-common, but the spray-painting charge threw me. I put on my protest face, looked him in the eye, and said nothing. I would remain silent even if he didn't read me my rights.

Officer Quast told me to hold my hands in front of me, snapped on handcuffs and thrust me into the backseat of an unmarked car. He drove down Bagby Street towards a blonde brick structure, the Houston city jail. Instead of going down the driveway where the new arrivals were dropped off, we headed around back to a line of one-story buildings.

He parked in a reserved parking spot and led me out of the car and through thick glass doors. Quast smiled and waved with one hand to the plainclothes officer we passed as he held me by the elbow, my wrists still handcuffed. It felt weirdly like we were impersonating an ordinary couple taking a stroll to cover a maniac leading his kidnapped victim to a basement dungeon.

We came to an office labeled CID headquarters. Quast opened the door for me to walk through, and pointed to a seat directly across from a desk. He sat down, pulled out a Polaroid camera, and snapped several close-up pictures of my face. I held on to my icy stare. Single sheets of exposed film churned out of the camera and developed as he lined them up on his desk. He stapled one to the outside of a manila folder, and threw the others into a drawer. After jotting down a few notes, he stood up and led me out the door, down a maze of passageways. We continued in silence, ending up in the women's side of the jail booking area. Quast took off the handcuffs and sat me down on a wooden bench. He walked to the partition separating the jailors from the jailed and announced, "Betty Sullivan is here."

The first thing I did was turn my hand over and check to see that Glen Van Slyke's phone number, written in black ink above my wrist, was still legible. I sighed with relief that the handcuffs didn't rub it off, and thought I should know by now to pick a less vulnerable place for such a valuable piece of information.

Glen was a lawyer with the National Lawyers Guild. He was a fierce defender of free speech and assembly and came to the rescue of activists being harassed by the police. Most of his professional work involved immigration law. Whether helping immigrants gain citizenship or rescuing radicals, he never lost a case. He was one of the few people I trusted who wore a suit.

Over the phone, my one phone call, Glen said someone would come to bail me out soon. Preparations were made before any protest or march to have a comrade or two stay home. They awaited a call if needed, from Glen, and were ready with cash and exact change, as we learned from experience, for bail.

I was taken to a small single cell and waited. If others from the demonstration were in cells close by, I had no way of knowing. It seemed like I was in a wing of the jail all by myself. After several hours passed, or half a day or I don't know how long, since I didn't wear my trusty watch to demonstrations, my name was called. I was removed from the cell and brought to the release area.

There was Glen. That was strange. Even if he made arrangements for bail, another comrade would pick me up. They couldn't all be still in jail, I hoped. I gave him a hug and thanked him for picking me up. I didn't feel a responsive soft pat on the back.

"This criminal mischief charge for spray-painting is a felony," he said. His crown of dense brown hair and matching mustache was expertly coiffed, a good cover for a lawyer with a radical heart.

"A felony?" I asked. "Why isn't it a misdemeanor? That's the only thing I've ever been charged with before."

"It's calculated on the cost of the damages. If the monetary loss to Exxon for the cleanup of the spray-painting is less than two hundred dollars, then it's a misdemeanor. If it is more, it's a felony."

"How much could it possibly cost to clean up spray-painting?"

"We'll find that out."

"I was home with Tony and Pete that night. I hate to lie, and if I did the spray-painting I would be honest with you."

Glen nodded his head and said, "Let's get out of here. Everyone else is bailed out. Nothing serious." We walked down the steps to the parking area.

My mind was whirling. Somehow I must have been mistaken for Maria. Tom told me she was with him at the Exxon building. Spray painting was a Revolutionary Youth thing. She was in her early twenties and I was thirty-one. I didn't volunteer any of that information to Glen. Being innocent, I wouldn't be found guilty of a crime I didn't commit. There was no reason to get sucked into being scared and save myself. And why should I?

No one, absolutely no one in the RCP or among its followers, spent significant time in jail, let alone prison. When three RCP supporters snuck into the Alamo, took down the Texas flag and raised the red flag, they were charged with disturbing the peace and only received a two hundred dollar fine. Members of People United to Fight Police Brutality, a group the RCP initiated after the Joe Torres murder, were charged with felony rioting after the Moody Park riot/rebellion. Tom was one of them, known as the Moody Park Three. They were initially charged with a total of one hundred forty years in prison and all of them got probation.

I had been arrested several times in the course of peaceful protests and it never amounted to anything. Not that I wanted to get arrested, but if what I was doing became illegal as a way to stop political activity, then avoiding being arrested was accepting those terms. Most of the time, getting arrested resembled a cat-and-mouse game with the police, part of the theatre of political action.

As Glen drove me home we made small talk about the recent basketball playoffs. Kareem Abdul-Jabaar was out with a sprained ankle, but rookie Magic Johnson led the Lakers to victory. Joe, my first husband and the kids' father, was a big basketball fan like Tom. Tony and Pete absorbed their interest, and I got into it, too. It was a rare family activity that didn't involve fighting the system, and because basketball was a game of the masses, it was politically correct.

As we turned onto my street, I felt confident that I had nothing to worry about. I was no big player in the scheme of things. I wasn't even in the RCP anymore. Glen would win another case, and the bad guys would lose. Politics aside, it was more my nature to be a Pollyanna than conjure up worst-case scenarios. The quote I chose to go with my high school yearbook picture, "The world is a wheel and it will all come round right," still had appeal. That same idealism led me to embrace "From each according to his ability to each according to his need," the famous slogan made popular by Marx.

Tom would have picked up Tony and Pete from daycare after work. They were such wonderful kids, trouping back and forth from our household to their father and stepmother's every week. They were close brothers. Sure they argued and could needle each other but it never escalated to hitting or punching one another.

Tom and I and Joe and Gail were on good terms. Tony and Pete were cherished by all of us. I was comforted that the children handled the disruption of a divorce and new stepparents so admirably.

Glen dropped me off at my house and said, "Don't worry, we'll get this all sorted out."

"I know we will," I said.

I had nothing to worry about.

# Chapter 2
# Justice Served

**Seven months later, December 8, 1981.**

The sign on the broad wooden door said, "185th Judicial District Court, Harris County." Glen pushed the unpolished brass handle and I followed him into the courtroom for the first of my six-day trial. The twelve-foot ceilings, offset by peeling crown molding, loomed above us. The walnut-brown bench for the judge and matching box for the jurors lay before us. I tightened my shoulder blades together, gaining another inch in height as we walked up the center aisle of the courtroom to the counsel's table on the right.

I sat down next to Bobby Caldwell, another lawyer volunteering his time to assist Glen. Bobby Caldwell was an African American with multiple sclerosis. His jerky grip squeezed my hand hello as his neck flinched to the side. I hoped the jury did not assume his body spasms were drink- or drug-induced.

I surveyed the prosecutors' table. Two men sat huddled together, flipping through stacks of paper. Assistant District Attorneys George Lambright and David Carlson. I would never keep them straight; both young, athletic-looking, clean-cut, hair just short of military.

From the back of the courtroom, the chatter grew louder. I turned to see two men. Morris Quast, the CID officer, I couldn't help but recognize. He was standing over a greying white man with khaki pants hitched up to his waist, head cushioned low and chin thrust forward.

"Who is that?" I asked Glen.

"Bob Price, the cab driver," he said.

"Really? For some reason I thought he would be younger." Tom didn't mention anything about what the cab driver looked like.

Bob Price and Officer Quast took seats in the first row behind the prosecutor's table as the bailiff entered the courtroom. "Hear ye, hear ye, hear ye. All rise for Judge George Walker."

Rise we did as the bald-headed judge entered the courtroom. He swept his long, black robe aside as he sat on his throne, surveying his domain. Judge Walker cracked his gavel down and said, "Court is in session. Please be seated."

The first order of business in a jury trial is picking the jury from a jury pool, a process called voir dire. Forty men and women, mostly white and middle-aged, filed into the courtroom and sat in the benches reserved for visitors when court is officially in session. Glen addressed the jury and started with the usual questions: What is your name? Where do you live? What do you do for a living? Can you render a verdict based on the facts of the case alone?

The members of the jury panel all answered affirmatively, relaxed and stretched back in their chairs. In the same matter-of-fact tone, Glen informed them of the felony criminal mischief charge for spray painting the Exxon building. As he attempted to disclose the content of the graffiti message, Assistant DA David Carlson shot up his hand and raised an objection.

"Ms. Sullivan is not on trial for what she painted on the building, but for the fact that she painted."

Judge Walker sustained his objection and instructed the defense to finish up their voir dire. All the questions Glen had prepared to ask potential jurors specifically about patriotism, military service, and their opinions about communism were left unanswered.

Assistant DA Carlson asked a few more questions, such as how long the potential jurors had lived in Houston, and reiterated to the jurors to consider only the facts of the case. He stated that the maximum sentence for felony criminal mischief was two years in prison. He smiled, looked at his watch and the judge, thanked the jury and sat down.

After the twelve-person jury was selected and seated in the jury box, the first witness, Bob Price, was called. After swearing "To tell the truth, the whole truth, and nothing but the truth, so help me God," he testified that he drove by the Exxon building in the early hours of the morning on April 28th and saw a woman spray-painting the wall. He stayed in his cab and watched as she completed, "Red, White, and Blue, We Spit on You, May Day, 1981."

Gasps escaped from every dropped jaw in the jury box. Bobby Caldwell jumped to his feet, waving his arms, and said, "I object."

Judge Walker stared down at the defense table and said, "Objection overruled. Please continue with the questioning."

I turned to Glen. His head was down. He was scribbling notes.

I couldn't make out what Glen was writing. I knew we didn't intend to hide the politics behind my arrest, but the jury was in no way prepared for this. We weren't either.

Bob Price continued: "After the woman finished spray painting, she came up to my cab and asked for a ride."

This seemed to me the craziest thing in the world. No one would write graffiti on a wall, turn around and ask a cab driver to give them a ride. I was ready to scream, "Can you actually believe this guy?"

But when I stole a glance at the jury in search of reassurance from the four men and eight women who held my fate, their eyes were turned to the witness stand, not a muscle moving. Taking it all in. As if swearing to tell the truth made it real.

Bob Price reported that he refused to give this woman a ride, got out of his car, grabbed her arm, and pulled her up the stairs to the entrance of the Exxon building. Meanwhile, a security guard ran out of the plate-glass doors, towards them. He faced Bob Price and told him to release the woman. Bob Price said he told the security guard about the spray-painting. Instead of asking for details, the security guard placed his hand on the gun in his holster and said, "I told you once already to let go of her." Bob Price loosened his grip on the woman, who then ran off. Bob Price pointed out the spray-painting on the wall of the building to the security guard and then called the police. The security guard was reportedly fired and never materialized again.

Bob Price testified that the next day a policeman named Officer Quast called him and arranged to meet him in the parking lot of a Popeye's chicken restaurant near downtown. Their "meeting" took place in Officer Quast's patrol car. Price testified that Quast brought a photo display of protest demonstrators and asked him to look through the pictures and see if he could identify the woman he saw writing on the wall of the Exxon building.

Most of the photos were long shots and it was hard to make out any individuals. In the few close-ups, more pictures of Betty Sullivan appeared than anyone else. Bob Price picked me out of the photo spread.

How did it happen that my picture was so prevalent? Bobbie Caldwell asked that question of Officer Quast: "Now, could you explain to the jury why a person of your experience would have three pictures of Betty Sullivan in the stack of pictures you carried out to Mr. Price?"

"You mean why I only had three pictures?" said Officer Quast.

"I mean why did you have three pictures of Miss Sullivan?"

"Because this is the individual that I believe to be the individual that Mr. Price described to me."

"Wasn't it suggestive by having that many in there?"

DA Carlson objected to this line of questioning. Judge Walker sustained his objection.

The last piece of the case against me was the cost of the removal of the spray paint. Paying four Exxon employees sixteen dollars an hour for eight hours to remove the graffiti with sandpaper added up to felony money. Especially in 1981, sixteen dollars an hour was extravagant pay for manual labor. It didn't raise any eyebrows on the jury. They looked ready for a nap when my lawyers meticulously questioned the efficiency of the materials and manpower used in the cleanup.

My time on the witness stand was coming up. The most ethical thing to do was stand up for my innocence without pretending I was somebody I was not. I was innocent. Mischief, even if criminal, was not a crime that hurt anyone.

I walked up to the witness seat next to the judge and sat down, trying hard to keep my body still without being rigid. Glen started off, asked me about my age, where I lived, my children. He asked me if I heard the testimony by Bob Price and asked if it was me who Bob Price saw painting the Exxon building on April 28th.

I answered: "No, it was not."

"Is there any doubt in your mind about that?"

"No, there is no doubt in my mind, whatsoever."

Off to my right side I heard a puzzling noise. Click, click, click. I couldn't tell where it was coming from or what it was. At the defense table I hadn't heard anything.

Glen cleared his throat and continued:

"Can you tell me where you were at that time on April 28th, 1981?"

"I was home with my children."

Click, click, and click again. Glen went on to ask me about the CID officers who provided Bob Price with the pictures of me for identification.

"Have you ever seen Officer Quast before?"

"I've seen him before, yes."

"You have. On how many occasions?"

"Over a dozen."

"Where did you have the occasion to see Officer Quast?"

"I've seen him, I guess you call it, I've observed him observing activities that I've been involved in, and that I've gone to. I've participated in some activities that the Revolutionary Communist Party has sponsored, some activities of Iranian students, of People United to Fight Police Brutality, things of that nature."

"What were you doing on those occasions?"

"Participating with people in demonstrations, rallies, or listening to speeches."

"Was Officer Quast participating in those demonstrations, rallies or speeches?"

"No, I wouldn't say he was participating in them."

"What was he doing at the time you saw him there?"

"He would take pictures or just watch."

"Have you ever seen him any other time other than when you were at a public demonstration?"

"I've been followed by him."

"When was that?"

"I remember in particular in 1979 before a demonstration that I didn't go to, there were two cars basically staked out on my street the whole morning. I'm pretty sure, but not positive, that he was in one of the cars."

"Has he ever followed you in his car?"

"Yes."

"What distance did he follow you on these occasions?"

"It would be a distance short enough where I would see him in my rearview mirror around every corner."

This was sounding good to me. The background clicking would start and stop but I was staying focused. Surely the jury was sympathetic to my exercising freedom of expression instead of the "secret police" spying on me.

Next I was cross-examined by Assistant DA George Lambright.

"I believe you stated, Miss Sullivan, that you have seen CID officers on numerous occasions in the past; is that not correct?"

"That's right."

"I believe you stated that you have seen them at the meetings you've gone to with reference to the Revolutionary Communist Party; is that correct?"

"That's right."

"Are you a member of the Revolutionary Communist Party, Miss Sullivan?"

Bobby Caldwell broke in: "Your honor, I'm going to object. It's totally irrelevant, as the State said in response to our voir dire on this case. Your Honor."

Judge Walker: "That's overruled."

"That's overruled?" said DA Lambright. "Thank you, Your Honor." (He turned towards me)

"Are you a member of that party?"

"No, I am not."

"Are you a member of the Communist Worker's Party?"

"No, I'm not."

Glen stood up: "Your Honor, I'm going to object to any more questions as to what political party Miss Sullivan is a member of. I thought she was on trial for allegedly damaging the Exxon Building and not for what political party she's a member of."

"That's overruled."

"Can you tell the ladies and gentleman of the jury then, Miss Sullivan, why you had an occasion to go to meetings of the Revolutionary Communist Party and have occasions to be seen there by CID officers?" said DA Lambright.

"Your Honor, I'm going to object to that question as being totally irrelevant to any issue as to the guilt or innocence of the defendant of the charge of criminal mischief of April 28, 1981," Glen interjected.

Judge Walker: "That's overruled."

Lambright continued: "What type of gatherings have you been to concerning the Revolutionary Communist Party?"

"I've been to forums, demonstrations. Mainly because I'm concerned about what's going on in the world and I want to be part of changing it and learn more about it."

"To the extent that you paint slogans on the side of the Exxon building?"

"No."

"I believe you have also stated that you've been to meetings and demonstrations regarding Iranian students. Is that not correct?"

"I've been to meetings to understand what their struggle is all about, in terms of the whole world, what people are doing and why."

"To the extent of painting slogans on a building, Miss Sullivan?"

"No."

"Your Honor, may we have a running objection in regards to this line of questioning?" asked Bobby Caldwell.

Judge Walker: "Yes sir, you may."

"Miss Sullivan, you heard the testimony to the effect that the slogan that was written on the Exxon building was 'Spit on you, red, white and blue, wave the red flag, May 1st,'" said Lambright.

"Yes."

"Would you attribute that as a communist slogan?"

"I don't know what type of slogan it is."

"Does May 1st have any meaning to you?"

"Yes, it does."

"Is it May Day?"

"Yes."

"And it's celebrated primarily by communists, is it not?"

"No, it's not."

"Do you know of any reason, Miss Sullivan, why a noncommunist would write the slogan that you saw depicted on the Exxon building?"

"I don't know why anybody would write any slogan on a wall, personally."

"No more questions for the witness."

I stood up from the witness stand and peered over to the judge's bench. A shiny metal nail clipper was on top of a legal pad.

As I was waiting to hear the jury's verdict, it struck me that no one on the jury had the experience of being a '60s radical, as I had. My activism was not about carrying guns and blowing up government targets. Would they have any idea that for me communism was an ideal, not a totalitarian state?

In the course of the trial, my previous arrests for disorderly conduct were disclosed. The jury could consider me a criminal. Or they could see my arrests as an intimidation tactic by the police. I didn't expect that they would agree with my politics, but could they respect me for putting my ideas into action? It was so obvious that I was set up by the police, that my political beliefs were on trial. Certainly the jury wouldn't consider my political beliefs reason enough for punishment.

Tom came to the trial when he wasn't scheduled to work at Whole Foods. We never discussed changing course and having him testify. As much as I mistrusted the system, the fact that I was innocent made it somehow inconceivable that I would be found guilty for something I didn't do. My lawyers vigorously defended me. It was obvious that the police manipulated Bob Price to identify me from photos. They practically admitted it! Spray-painting was not a serious crime, even if they called it a felony. It was hype. What could it possibly amount too? And if Tom got involved, he was the one who had more at stake, still being on probation as former Moody Park Three. How could he point the finger at Maria without saying he was part of the spray-painting too? Now if Maria would have come forward when this all started . . . But she didn't and neither did he.

Any fear I had was quickly dismissed. As I write this it seems implausible that I didn't consider that I was indeed taking the fall for a crime I didn't commit and there could be consequences beyond my control. Instead I applauded myself for being immune to any panic and felt assured that my life would not be turned upside-down

December 21, we all piled back into the courtroom. Robert Obenhaus, the foreman of the jury, handed the written verdict to Judge Walker, which he read out loud. "We, the jury, find the defendant guilty as charged."

I felt faint. Felt shivers. Felt like throwing up. But reason prevailed. It was a shock; it was injustice. I'd be on probation. I could handle that.

The punishment phase was next. My attorney brought forth witnesses to attest to my good character. One of them was Beverly Gallo the manager at the Bennigan's where I worked as a waitress after leaving the Post Office and during my trial.

Bobby Caldwell asked her: "Do you realize that this jury found Miss Sullivan guilty of felony criminal mischief and she could face two years in prison?"

"Yes, that is what I've been told."

"And are you familiar with the alleged facts?"

"No, sir. The only thing I know is that Betty was supposedly having problems with painting something. I never got the whole story until now."

"Well, you realize that she's now convicted of painting on the Exxon building."

"Yes."

"If you heard that the jury found Miss Sullivan guilty of writing a slogan, 'Red, white, and blue, we spit on you, fly the red flag on May Day,' would you change your opinion in regards to anything you stated in regards to Miss Sullivan?"

"No."

"Having the conviction of this offense, would Betty still have a job with you if this jury would see fit to grant her probation?"

"Yes, I do."

In the cross-examination Mr. Lambright asked Ms. Gallo if she knew about my previous arrests and if that would change her opinion of my reputation. She answered no. He then asked, "If she does a good job for you, she could go out and kill somebody, and she will still have a good reputation for being peaceful and law abiding?"

She answered: "I am not interested in Betty's private life as long as she carries on in our restaurant as a law-abiding person."

I was the final witness in the punishment phase. Bobby Caldwell ended his questioning with: "You are telling the jury that if they would see fit in their hearts to be merciful towards you and your two children, let you go back to work and take care of these two kids, that whatever contract you'll make with the Court, you'll keep?"

"Yes," I answered.

DA Lambright was the last to cross-examine me.

"Miss Sullivan, do you realize that in order to revoke someone's probation, that first they have to commit an offense; they have to violate their probation?"

"Yes."

"Number two, there have to be witnesses to that violation; isn't that correct?"

"Right."

"Number three, a motion to revoke your probation has to be filed."

"Yes."

"Number four, you have to be brought into court, along with the witnesses, and there has to be a hearing before the judge."

"Yes."

"And number five, the Judge, if he desires, revokes your probation, if he sees fit; correct?"

"Right."

"And then you are punished for the offense that you were convicted of in the past."

At this point I was wondering why any jury would bother with probation.

The jury was asked if they wanted to quit for the day or go ahead and render a verdict on my punishment. They decided to get it over with.

"Having found the defendant guilty of criminal mischief, we assess her punishment at confinement in the Texas Department of Corrections for a period of two years."

I couldn't believe it. A surge of confusion filled my brain. I didn't feel anything but numbness. My years as a communist trained me to focus on the world. I had no way to understand what was going on inside myself. Going to prison was beyond my comprehension, and comprehension was all I had.

Glen and Bobbie drew their arms around me. I felt like a block of ice despite their warm embrace. Their comfort turned to anger. The conviction was irrational. Going to prison for spray painting was outrageous.

As if reading my mind, Glen told me there were plenty of grounds for appeal—the voir dire was cut short, the suggestive photo display. The trial was only the first step. Bobbie said they would get started with the appeal right away. I shouldn't worry.

Tom stood at the back of the courtroom. I walked away from the defense table to him. We hugged. He looked like he'd seen a ghost.

# Chapter 3
# Appeals

Glen and Bobby's appeal of my case consisted of six grounds for error, as they are called. The two main points were: number one, "The trial court erred in restricting the Appellant's voir dire examination of the jury venire panel so severely that her counsel were unable to intelligently exercise Appellant's peremptory challenges"; number two, "The trial court denied Appellant the right of due process of law by permitting the in-court identification of Appellant Bob Price, the sole witness connecting her with the offense, because there was no clear and convincing evidence that his in-court identification was not tainted by a pre-trial display of photographs which was so impermissibly suggestive as to create a substantial likelihood of mistaken identification by the witness."

An amicus brief was filed by the American Civil Liberties Union, ACLU. Their interest in the case came from the concern that my association with the RCP motivated my arrest, not the actual spray painting. If the message had been "God Bless America" or "Nuke Iran," the brief pointed out, the state would not have devoted the same efforts to apprehending and punishing the author of the spray-painting.

The brief described the average American citizen's strong attachment towards the flag. With limited voir dire, the extent of potential prejudice of prospective jurors was not discovered. Appellant's counsel, they wrote, was not allowed to ask questions about the content of the painted message and seek out potential jurors' attitudes to that content that would reflect their attitude toward me.

In my mind, as well as the lawyers', the appeals had legal standing. There were favorable rulings that pertained to my case. Citing those rulings is the method by which appeals go about proving errors. The eyewitness identification from photographs, a suggestive photograph display at that, was gaining recognition nationally as unreliable. It didn't seem like we were unrealistic to think that the appeals would go my way.

I reminded myself about the RCP action at the Alamo that made headlines just a year before my arrest. Those charges were quickly resolved without a trial or jail time. It could be that the powers in charge wanted to shut down any potential publicity around the Alamo. If they had a trial, the RCP would surely organize protests. My case, on the other hand, was not in the news. At least not when I was arrested and tried. That would come later. Since leaving the RCP, I would no longer benefit from them taking my case to the streets, as they say. I was frankly relieved about that. Then I began to wonder: if I had been in the RCP, would that attention have helped me or hurt me? That I was even thinking about the RCP helping or hurting my chances of staying out of jail was a revelation in itself. Before, it would have been all about what would help or hurt the cause, not my personal circumstances.

There was nothing to do but await the results of the appeal process. Try to live a normal life. Reversal of the charges seemed the most logical outcome. No reason to be scared.

# Chapter 4
# Descent

**November 14, 1985. Four long years later.**

I stood in front of the refrigerator, contemplating what was on the other side of the door to cook for supper when the phone rang. Glen was on the other end.

"I hate to give you the bad news, but your last appeal was denied by the Texas Supreme Court. They voted four to one against you. The one minority argument was very positive. The suggestive photo display hit a nerve. I'll send you a copy of their ruling. We may appeal to the U.S. Supreme Court! In the meantime, I'm so sorry, you can't stay free on bond any longer."

Glen, optimistic through the years of the appeal process. The Supreme Court, still holding out hope. But all the appeals, like chemo, didn't save the patient. Lawyers, like doctors, hate to lose.

I thanked Glen, told him how much I appreciated everything he did and dropped the phone. I couldn't move. My calf muscles seized up. Then they trembled. I grabbed onto one of the kitchen chairs. It felt like a trap door opened and I was falling and falling with nothing to catch me. Saliva started pooling on my tongue, and I was afraid I'd start foaming at the mouth. I didn't want Tom or especially the kids to see me in this state. I slid off to the bedroom, put my head under the pillow, and curled up in the fetal position. With my eyes closed, a vision of that Edgar Allan Poe story, "The Pit and the Pendulum," filled my mind. The Pendulum's sharp blade was coming closer and closer and my hope for rescue was getting dimmer and dimmer. I could feel myself shaking. The idea of fleeing the country that some acquaintance suggested seemed the perfect solution, but how could I do that with a husband and two young children? I wondered what had ever happened to Maria. Was she still in the Revolutionary Youth Brigade? Since Tom and I were outsiders, we had no contact with the RCP other than with Joe and Gail, and that was because of the kids. Tony and Pete spent weekdays with Tom and me and weekends with Joe and Gail. Even though Joe was their biological father, the one time we all got together to talk about that remote possibility that I would go to jail, we agreed to keep the same arrangement. It would keep things as usual for the kids. Joe and Gail thought it was safer that way too. There was persistent concern that those still aligned with the RCP continued to be under some kind of surveillance. I could have stayed in bed for hours trying to figure out the future, trying to figure out the past, but I needed to face the present.

I sat up straight, smoothed down my shirt with my clammy hands, licked my lips, and stepped out of the bedroom. I sucked in my breath and tried to appear composed as I entered the living room and sat down next to Tom, who was on the couch.

"That was Glen on the phone. He said my final appeal was denied."

Tom's arms encircled me. I let out a long moan and pulled back.

"I have to tell the kids."

"Yes," he said. "They should know we aren't hiding anything from them."

We both got up and called Tony and Pete in from playing outside. They came in through the kitchen door. Gathered in the kitchen, I placed my hands over my stomach to suppress the gurgling and found a small voice.

"I just heard from the lawyer that my appeal was denied. There is nothing more they can do right now. I have to go to jail." A hush sucked the air out of the room. We all grabbed each other and hugged so tightly I could barely breathe. I was barely breathing anyway.

I never believed this day would come. Never. Who the hell goes to prison for spray-painting? I didn't even do it. I didn't do it. I didn't matter.

# Chapter 5
# The Pit

Screams, crying, cursing, banging on the thick bars. Women moaning, sobbing, staring into space, curled on mattresses on the floor, somehow sleeping through the mayhem. The air was dense and suffocating. Legs and arms of all shades of the human race pushing and stepping over each other just to maneuver around. I was transported into a Hieronymus Bosch painting.

The initial bombardment subsided as I categorized this new presence—part refugee camp, part animal pen. This pit was a large rectangular dormitory, a women's group cell at the Harris County jail.

There were twenty-four bunk beds for close to forty women. Mattresses were scattered between the bunks, leaving skinny paths to walk through. Off to the side was a bathroom area. There were three toilets in a row separated by narrow partitions on each side. There weren't any doors. The front opened up to the guard-patrolled hallways. I walked closer and saw a woman crouched down, sitting on the pot. I turned away from her and noticed two shower stalls with clear plastic shower doors. I shuddered, thinking about being naked in front of the other women and guards. Privacy was another freedom we were stripped of.

There was a smaller dayroom with a blaring TV hanging from the ceiling and a long line at the pay phone on the wall next to it. Little wonder the women were shouting into the phone. The noise and crush of bodies was smothering. There were many black women but no shortage of whites and Hispanics.

In this jumble of chaos my instinct was to stand there, immobile. It seemed an eternity before the animated sound of a few women chatting among themselves pierced my frozen state.

"Did you hear that crazy lady say she shot her husband but had three boyfriends over seventy-five years old?"

"Do you believe she rolls up her trick money, then stashes it in her pussy, like she claims?"

"The jail guards didn't lift a finger to help that poor bitch with the heavy withdrawal from heroin last night. What about the two women who had miscarriages here two nights ago? That got everyone up in arms."

My ears picked up on a childlike voice saying to a younger woman, "I'm only thirteen, but I'd rather be charged with prostitution as an adult, or I'll get sent to a youth institute until I'm sixteen."

Another woman said, "Hey Josephine, you in here again? Did you see your homegirl, Francie? She here too."

"Yeah, I saw her, and the bitch cousin of hers that can't keep away from the needle."

It was horrifying to hear these pieces of stories. I wasn't frightened as much as feeling out of my element. The woman didn't seem threatening. It was more like being invisible on a battlefield. I was watching a scene and was in it at the same time. And it seemed like everyone knew everyone else. Except for me. I searched for someone I could connect with and nearly bumped into a light-skinned black woman squatting on the floor, writing a letter. She looked my way and must have sensed that I wasn't like so many of the others for whom jail was a familiar experience. She rose to her feet, pushing up from the floor with a groan. Her name was Pat.

"It's hard to get to use the telephone and sometimes the guards turn it off to punish us. They say we make too much of a racket. But they pick up mail every day. I'm writing my favorite grandson. I've taken care of him since he was a baby and he knows that I didn't write those bad checks on purpose. Just can't always make ends meet. I'm hoping he can round up enough money to bail me out of here after payday."

"The guards didn't tell me anything about letters. That's great to know."

She snickered. "Don't count on the guards telling you anything. They call us ladies, but treat us like dirt. They won't even give you the time of day. The lights stay on 24/7, and with no clocks, people coming and going at all hours, you can't tell day from night. You learn to tell time by the meals and roll call."

"No way to tell time?" I had always worn a watch and was fanatically punctual. The ground was slipping away from me.

"But don't look so worried," she said. "You'll be fine. We really do help each other out. We're all in this together, and misery loves company. We all miss our kids and have that in common."

"I have kids, too," I muttered to myself.

I didn't want to lose Pat and gathered all my courage to initiate a conversation.

"Tell me about your family." I asked.

A small smile spread on Pat's face as her speech slowed.

"I have one grown son and three grandkids, but their mother's the problem. Got hooked on drugs. What did I do to deserve a daughter-in-law like that?"

"Sorry to hear that," I said.

"Don't be sorry for me. Nothing I can't handle. I have high hopes for the grandchildren. That's what keeps me going. I tend to spoil them. Of all things to land in jail for, hot checks, can you imagine? The grandson I'm writing to is a senior at Westbury High School, works on the weekends. I know he's on the right track. My son is doing the best he can."

I nodded, afraid anything coming out of my mouth would sound patronizing. After a long silence, Pat went back to writing her letter. I had no idea what to do with myself but watch Pat. If only I had paper and pencil. A letter would be my magic carpet and fly me away from here. Pat's eyes followed mine. "Take this. It will make you feel better." She handed me two sheets of her paper and a nub of a pencil she had in her bra.

"Thank you, Pat, you're so kind. You don't know how much I appreciate this." Tears gushed from my eyes. There was no way to hold them back.

"Stop blubbering, girl. It's only a little paper and half a pencil," she said.

With Pat's supplies I sunk to the floor and started my first letter to Tom and my kids. So much had happened in so little time. I needed that lifeline to my old world to keep my sanity, which, until that day, I had never doubted. My brain was a pinball bumping from flipper to flipper as I clutched on to my paper, starting and stopping the letter, clearing a space in my head, making sense of the swirling world. As day and night truly had no meaning, whenever exhaustion took over I collapsed on some surface and welcomed the oblivion of sleep.

*November 22, 1985*
*Dearest Sweethearts,*

*I'm fortunate to have been able to borrow all the equipment for this letter. My heart is breaking, writing this to you, because I miss you all so much. I try not to think about it. It's still all very new and I feel very vulnerable so I sort of bounce from holding back tears and the thoughts of all of you, and try to figure out my new jail identity. There is a tremendous sense of common suffering and need to somehow make it tolerable through sharing and compassion. Another side is people just acting wild and posing, as I guess a way to let the rage out.*

*Everyone pretty well stands up for themselves. You have to push forward if you want or need anything. But everyone is basically respectful of one another. Especially being so new, I know I'll have to learn the ropes and probably have to toughen up some.*

*Not a lot of bullshit gets by. Being too "nice" can give the wrong impression. I'm learning little by little how to act, how far to go or not go. I have to resist crawling into my shell and being miserable, but it's a struggle. You kind of have to define yourself, your space, in jailhouse terms. It's funny, there's all sorts of slang for things that I have yet to catch on to.*

*Before I get any deeper, let me tell you two things. I'm never sure if I can use the phone. It is sort of by appointment and I'm on the low end of the totem* pole. Except my "crime" and TDC time gives me some respect—or pity. The other is: Tom, could you please put $10.00 in my inmate trust fund? You should do it ASAP because all the processing with the holidays will really hold things up and I need to buy shampoo etc. not to mention letter-writing stuff. You can't send stamps but maybe an extra slice of stationery with a letter will add to my paper supply. My address MUST BE JUST SO.

Betty Sullivan
spm#386267 cellblock #4-C-2
Harris County Jail
1301 Franklin St.
Houston, Texas 77002

And you have to have a complete return name and address in the upper left-hand corner for me to receive mail.

. . . It is noisy all the time here . . . so fluid, people's interacting tensions building and calming, the confusion of the bureaucracy, the TV on nonstop and so much time to fill. Everyone is fairly grounded and accessible; of course they all seem a bit crazed and resigned . . . This is such a mind trip, what a roller coaster I am on . . . Maybe I'll get a sexual education here.

Actually this letter is making me feel better. When I pick up a pencil, it's our way of touching. At least every day will get me closer to the end, but right now it's the hardest because I have so little behind me. Basically I can't wait to get through the day and escape through sleep. Hope this is not depressing you too much . . .

*Oh guys, I can't tell you how much I love you. I'll try not to dwell on self-pity. I guess the hurt won't stop, but it will be better when I can work into the fabric of life here. I'll be more an inmate and not feel so awful when I think of the outside world. But don't think I feel distant. I feel entirely in your hearts and minds.*

*My love is forever with you,*
*Betty*

It seemed impossible that I jam-packed those experiences into a letter. It seemed impossible that all of that happened in one day. Or one night. One day-night. Time expanded and contracted without any reference point.

It was only a few days ago that Glen told me when he called that I could either turn myself in or wait to be picked up by the police. I wasn't going to have the police knocking on my door in the middle of the night to drag me away. Knowing the date to surrender, I would have some control. Control, ha!

My previous arrests had brought me to the Houston City Jail where people are bailed out quickly or moved to the Harris County Jail. I had never been to the county jail and had no idea what to expect. The only thing I knew was that at some point I would be transferred to the women's penitentiary in Gatesville. To the non-con, the city jail, the county jail, and state and federal prison may seem like interchangeable terms. They are not.

Anyone getting arrested from the street, in their car, or at their home is taken by the police to the city jail, the giant dustpan where those left behind by society get swept up and deposited at one point or another—or over and over. The city jail provides the barest accommodations for the highest turnover. Once charges are filed, which is usually within twenty-four hours, you are eligible for bail. This is a way to let you out of jail yet guarantee that you show up for hearings and/or trial. If you are arrested for a minor crime, bail is set between $500 and $2,000. If families can come up with this amount of money, they pay a "cash bond." The full amount of money is returned when your case is resolved.

When the crime is more serious, the bail is higher. If you and your family don't have access to thousands of dollars, you turn to a bail bondsman. In exchange for securing you bond, the bail bondsman requires a percentage of the bail and collateral, as with cars or property. You never get the percentage back, even if you comply with all legal proceedings. If you skip out on a bail bond, there is not only a warrant out for your arrest, but bounty hunters hired by the bail bond company to track you down. If this sounds scary and like something out of an old-time western, it is.

Prison is another place, another society, an institution with its own cultures and traditions. Think: going away to UT instead of commuting to Houston Community College from home. The minimum prison sentence is two years; most are for crimes against the state, thus served in state prisons. Federal prison is reserved for spies, mobsters and white-collar criminals. City, county, state and federal prisons are different in environment and experiences.

My incarceration started by turning myself in to authorities at the county jail, where I'd await transfer to Gatesville State Prison. I remembered that day and the turmoil I felt leaving my kids, as if I was living in that moment. It was November 21, 1985, a week before Thanksgiving.

Visions of roasted turkey and Southern-style cornbread stuffing that I was so proud to have mastered dissolved. No matter how feverishly I blocked thoughts of being away from my family for all the upcoming holidays, they hung on like a stain. At the time, Tony was ten-and-a-half and Pete eight. I begged to believe that they could somehow understand that my absence was only temporary and that when it would be over, it would all be over with. For good.

My vulnerable young children, vulnerable but hardly sheltered. They were "red diaper babies." The phrase refers to children born to left-leaning parents. These kids, as their appalled grandparents reported, objected to eating American cheese and didn't root for the USA when watching the Olympics. I heard all about it. I couldn't imagine why they preferred the "International" to the "Star-Spangled Banner."

We weren't teaching them to be UN-American. It was the economic system that we were against. The people and the government were not the same. The working people of the world. That was where our allegiance was.

Joe and I, and later Tom and Gail, considered having children in our lives as essential. We read Tony and Pete bedtime stories, played in the park, and had birthday parties like normal families. But the other stuff, the activist culture, was the core of our lives. The kids spent time in group-babysitting with other comrades and their children, while their parents darted from one meeting or protest to another.

We had sense enough to refrain from taking them anywhere we thought dangerous, but little sense of how they perceived our activities and the dangers we took for granted, little sense of how they felt being eclipsed by the all-encompassing class struggle. It wasn't something that crossed my mind. In my world children were resilient. They would understand. At that time I saw myself as protector of my children, by looking out for their larger interests in promoting a more just world. Any question of how my priorities would affect them, how they needed security in their day-to-day world, was so deeply buried as to be nonexistent. Yet I never felt anything less than unconditional love for them, and being a mother was an integral part of my identity.

With the prospect of being sent away to prison, I never knew how much or how little to tell my kids. They were older than when I was first arrested. I wanted to shelter them but I also thought hiding the truth would serve only a temporary purpose. Explaining to your kids that their mother is going to jail was not a chapter in Dr. Spock's baby book.

In the days leading up to my incarceration, I reminded myself that I had spent time in jail, if only a few hours. The women were more depressed than anything else. I wasn't scared for my life. What was scary was being taken away. Removed. Exiled. How would my family do without me? How would I do without them?

When the morning of Thursday, November 21, arrived, I rose to start this different day in my usual way, with a morning shower. Allowing myself to linger longer than normal, I lavishly washed my hair and put on an extra dab of conditioner. I shaved my legs and armpits.

Who knows when or how they do showers in jail? I probably wouldn't see a razor anytime soon. I hadn't let my body hair grow since the '60s. Back then I thought shaving was an unnecessary pain. I still did, but had come to feel more obliged to conform to society's norms. Certainly nobody gets a razor in jail. I smiled to myself, thinking of the irony that I could enjoy that little freedom of letting my body hair grow while the rest of me would be imprisoned.

I turned off the water, stepped out of the shower stall, dried myself off, and wrapped a bath towel around my torso. Looking in the mirror I wondered about haircuts. I couldn't imagine my long, thick red hair, my best feature, being chopped off. Dressed in my trusty Mexican house dress, I tried to force down a few bites of shredded wheat and fruit. My last meal. When would I get to eat fresh fruit again? Would I get that sticky concoction of pale pink and yellow cubes called fruit cocktail? I was lucky to have lots of fresh veggies and fruit growing up and liked to eat healthy. Would I be able to stomach jail food? Would I lose weight or get fat? The crisis of going to jail had zeroed in on my body. I separated my heart. That would stay at home.

I hastily got dressed. It was absurd to waste time worrying about what to wear to jail, and I was never concerned about what to wear anyway.

I couldn't believe this. I felt rage starting to swell up in me. Maria never came forth to tell the truth. Yet at the time there was no reason for her to come forward. Spray painting wouldn't result in a prison sentence. I wouldn't rat on another comrade. What kind of comrade would that make me?

But here I was going to prison. She saved herself. Isn't that what people are supposed to do? I had kids; didn't I think about their welfare? Shouldn't I save myself for them? I cursed her with a lifetime of guilt and shame but those retaliatory thoughts didn't make me feel any better.

There would be plenty of time in jail to stew and sort things out. My impulse was to embed these last moments of freedom into my memory. I looked around one final time. Squinting through tears, and with all the intensity I could bring to bear, I forced down as many details of my modest home and beautiful, innocent kids as I could.

My mind was a hard rubber ball, not the sponge I wanted it to be. There was no place in my traumatized brain for those flashes of my old life to cling to. Leaving home was a blur. The kids: where were they? I only remember Tom driving me in that same VW Rabbit to downtown Houston. By the time we got there, I could concentrate on my surroundings, slow it down and drink in the world.

Traffic. Trucks and city buses fought over the road. Tom parked the car in a sprawling city surface lot. Men in dark suits and hard hats rubbed shoulders crossing the street. Pigeons pecked at discarded fast food wrappers thrown from the curb. Everyone and everything had a place to go and a job to do. Our private agenda was so out of step as we approached the ten-story-tall Harris County Jail.

You wouldn't know that this drab, tan building was a jail unless you had business there. There is no sign that says county jail outside the building. This place was out of sight and out of mind to all except those it held captive.

A policeman held open a thick, metal door as Tom and I walked into a closet-like receiving area. That was the last male in uniform I would see. We were told by a female jail guard to wait for instructions. Standing there, Tom and I shared a look at my left hand. Jewelry was not allowed in jail. I remembered to leave the watch I wore every day at home. My wedding ring. That was so much a part of me I didn't even think of it as jewelry. I slid off the gold band from my ring finger and handed it to Tom. He took the ring and clenched it in his fist. Another guard approached from an unseen doorway and told us it was time for me to go. Tom's body enclosed me one last time, sobbing and whimpering, I let go of him as the guard officially took custody of me.

"Turn around and put your hands behind your back," she said and proceeded to lock handcuffs on my wrists. One last look at the back of Tom with his hands reaching deep into the rear pocket of his jeans, and I was led away to the booking area.

An incredible tug of exhaustion took over. I wasn't merely out of focus; I was in a complete fog and felt all my mental capacities shutting down. My head bobbed and my eyes rolled back. Holding my head up as I dragged my feet to keep up with the guard was more effort than I could imagine.

Somehow the handcuffs were removed. I was searched and motioned to sit on a bench, my limp body nearly sliding to the floor. I was unaware if I was alone or with others. Nodding off and on, I was guided to a long, wooden counter where my fingerprints were taken. Fingers inked and pressed, I was told to make a quarter-turn. Flash. Blink. My mug shot was taken. I signed papers with fuzzy letters I could barely read. The guard led me to a small dressing room. She handed me what looked like a faded house dress, cotton underwear and flip flop slippers. I slapped my face to wake up enough to change into the jail garb. All of my free-world clothes were stuffed in a bag and whisked away. To my amazement I was given a razor along with a toothbrush and toothpaste. Apparently the powers that be considered shaving a necessary part of daily life. How could it be more important to allow women to shave than to worry about what they might do with a razor, even a safety razor? Without the civility of shaving, would hordes of women covered with previously unseen body hair revert back to a more voracious primal state? That thought sparked a vision of a Planet of the Apes-like jail revolt. At least I was conscious enough to amuse myself.

After all my admission requirements were completed, I was escorted by two guards through a maze of long, grey, concrete corridors. I was pitched inside a new reality as a gigantic clank of heavy, metal doors locked behind me.

# Chapter 6
# Lifeline

The next forty-eight hours in the county jail, I bobbled between pretending that I was still home and this was a bad trip and trying to get my bearings. A fear of drowning plagued me. The floor was solid concrete, I knew that, but walking on it was like quicksand. I couldn't catch my breath. The dizzy motion of women darting around felt like vertigo. The only antidote to the spinning was keeping Pat in my sight. She was my reference point. Without Pat, a dead sleep was my escape, which unfortunately never lasted long on the floor. Later I would inherit a spot on a top bunk from one of ladies who got bailed out. Those few feet of bony mattress were salvation. I wished I could spend twenty-four hours scrunched down in my escape capsule. It was impossible.

Out of nowhere I heard my name called. It was a guard standing on the other side of the cell door. I sprang up and, having no idea what was going on, followed her out of the cell, down a bleak network of hallways and elevators. I arrived in a room filled with women inmates sitting behind a long counter, facing a Plexiglas wall. Guards were positioned every few feet behind them. I was handed off and motioned to sit on a chair between two other inmates. There was a grimy phone receiver connected to the wall. On the other side of the Plexiglas, holding an identical receiver, sat Tom.

"Oh, God, Tom, I can't believe it. How did you get here?"

"I was so worried I wouldn't make it, but I'm here. I can't believe it either. Didn't anyone tell you about visitors?

"No, they don't tell me anything."

"I found out I could visit you if I brought our marriage certificate, which wasn't the easiest thing to find. But you need to put people on a list. All our friends want to visit you. The kids too."

"How are Tony and Pete? I love them and miss them so much. My heart aches whenever I think of them."

"They're great. I'm calling them the champions of the world. I don't know if it has really sunk in yet. It's hard for me."

"I'm just so glad to see you. I still can't believe it," I said. And I cried and cried. The rest of the visit was Tom telling me everything was going to be alright and to put everyone on the visitor list while I cried and nodded.

Our fifteen minutes of visitation ended. As a guard led me back towards the exit door, I turned my head and watched Tom watch me being taken out of the visitor room. Seeing Tom, it was the first miracle of jail. I don't believe in miracles. But I can't think of any other word that better describes what it felt like. Those first days of jail, I was dissolving. Melting. Disappearing. Vanishing. Seeing Tom brought me back to life. If I could keep hold of the outside world while I was inside this unreal reality, I would be OK.

*November 23, 1985*
*Dearest Betty,*

*It was so good to see you tonite (sic). I can't express it. You just looked radiantly beautiful. Please don't think I'm trying to make you feel good. I'm telling the truth. Absence makes me thirsty for your presence, touch, and talk. It was the day before yesterday they took you. Seems like a week. Time has palpably slowed. I know you are strong and that your crying is triggered by my presence, so tho I'm worried and think about you constantly, don't think I'm thinking that you're just crying all the time.*

*The kids have been so good. God, they are magnificent young human beings. They cleared the table, set the pans to soak, did their homework, and sorted the laundry all by themselves (Tony's initiative). We folded the clothes together (Tony and I), which included some of your shirts and underwear, and they just seemed so poignant, radiating "not-there-ness." It was a struggle not to succumb to self-pity, but there's so much necessity that that's not the biggest problem. Tony's button fell off his dark grey pants so I sewed on the button from the back pocket—but your sewing bag, too, broadcasts your absence. I know we can handle this. But it seems like the roaches are bigger.*

*We had rancheros fiesta and tofu with fruit salad tonite—AUGH, that's you too. We had pumpkin pie for a treat, read Peter Churchmouse, and then bed . . . When I got home, Gary had called and was outraged and anxious to help. So I directed him to Jack. They're going to do some stuff together . . . It sounds quite real. I'm amazed. It's a damn groundswell. And it's totally out of our hands. It is becoming a civil liberties issue... Without getting too emotional about it, I feel pretty strongly that these forces going in our favor will have their effect. It's the first time I actually feel positive about any facet of this predicament in the last four years . . . What can I say Betty love? You are right here with us. If there is anything we can do for you, please speak. We all love you so much.*

*Stay strong,*
*Tom*

My new mission was to find out how to put people on the visitor list. Pat was my portal into the workings of jail, and she told me I needed to get a visitor list form from one of the guards who paraded the hallway outside of the cell. I waited by the entrance. Where are the guards when you need one? At last one came by. Raising my voice above the noise in the cell, I yelled out, "Can I get a visitor list . . . please?" The guard drew a crumpled form out of her pocket, handed it to me through the cell bars, and told me to write down names and addresses and phone numbers of no more than ten people. I didn't have all that memorized, but names emptied out of me: Tom and Tony and Peter, Kelly and Beth and Jack, Josie, and more. Writing down that list reminded me of how much support I had, how many people cared. It was more than I could ask for.

A few days later, when the guard came into the dorm and called my name again, I knew what to expect. I practically skipped to the visiting room. When I plopped down on the rigid chair, I opened a crack in my senses and took it all in: the smell of sweat, the kick marks on the walls, the bright, fluorescent bulbs, some dead; the

Plexiglas wall dividing the inmate side from the visitor side was streaked with fingerprints; the sticky telephone receivers. Did they ever disinfect those things?

This time it was Josie who sat across from me. We met at a Fundamentals of Drawing class at the Glassell School in Houston. When I was growing up, my best friend Lynn's mother entertained us with art supplies. She was an artist herself, yet relegated to substitute art teacher while she raised a family in suburban Long Island, New York. I don't think I had any unique gift for art, but being exposed at a young age to real paints by her mom, and more traditional knitting supplies by my mom, instilled in me a lifelong desire to make things. I took the art class with Josie while my appeals were still going on and I was working at Texas Art Supply. It was one of the rare moments in that time period of taking initiative to see what I wanted to do with the rest of my life. The art class convinced me that being serious about art was harder than I envisioned. Many people in the class were way better at art than me. It was even a bit discouraging, but also a good introduction to what it means to see as an artist. Meeting Josie was what made it all worthwhile. We became friends. She was a graphic artist and had a flexible schedule. When I went to jail, she came to visit me regularly.

Before anyone from the public is allowed in the jail's visitors area, they are subject to a pat down or more thorough search. Josie told me that when she came to see me, there was a young black man wearing a leather jacket ahead of her. He was taken out of the line and searched. She wore a fluffy, goose-down coat, and said she could have hid any numbers of things, yet she went through the line with barely a hand on her. She said it made her realize how much image affects how one is treated in the world. I was so glad that visiting me provided her with personal insights into the inequality so prevalent in the criminal justice system she wouldn't get otherwise.

We talked about Luis, her Mexican American boyfriend, who she hoped would be her future husband and father to the children she was craving. They were thinking about moving in together. He told her she lent him some respectability, which wasn't something she wanted to be known for.

Any time my friends visited, I was reminded that getting to jail was no small feat. You can't get to downtown Houston in less than twenty minutes from anywhere. Finding a parking space. Getting cleared by security. Making sure your name is on the visitor list. Showing identification. Waiting in line. Waiting in line some more. Wondering how extensively you will be searched. All the while inhaling secondhand smoke streaming off of people's clothing. This could take three times longer than the fifteen minutes allotted to actually visit with someone in jail.

As time passed I kept myself from literally jumping for joy when the guard came for me at visiting time every night, because there was someone there for me. Every night. My family and friends would not let one day go by without somebody set up to visit. It was another miracle.

I felt guilty. No one else in jail had so many people on the outside holding them up. Then again, they seemed to have outside people inside with them. Still I was self-conscious and slinked off with the guard, keeping my head down while my heart beat with elation and gratitude.

Sometimes my children came to visit with Tom. Tom would take turns holding each of them on his lap to let them speak into the receiver. Pete would stammer when he started to talk to me, but with Tom's long arms around him, his voice would smooth out. Tony was always more verbal, but soon his eyes would get red and I knew it was time for them to go. I dug my fingernails into the palm of my hand, causing enough pain to distract me from the torture of seeing them leave. I held back the torrent of tears until they turned their backs and headed out. I made sure they left before me, so I could watch them instead of the other way around.

I longed to be near my children, and seeing them lifted my spirits like nothing else. If Tom was my anchor, Tony and Pete were my lifeline. They were the only thing I was proud of, even if I wasn't proud of not putting them first. I didn't know whether jail visits would add to the trauma of me being gone, but I couldn't imagine surviving without seeing them. I hadn't thought about how they would see me.

There were no mirrors in jail. I didn't know whether I looked like the madwoman I felt I was. Bringing my kids to this scary place, seeing this scary woman whom they called Mommy, would scare me too.

I blotted that out of my mind. I thought it would be better for them to see me than to wonder where I was. Tom agreed. Shielding them from coming to jail would make me invisible. My physical presence was better than some ghost. But I wondered if that was a convenient excuse to make myself feel better. Seeing them, hearing their voices, knowing they were there, was something I needed. I didn't think I could live without those visits. Was my self-preservation making the rules?

I came to terms with the fact that at one time, I thought the revolution was more important than any individual. That included myself and everyone I loved. That included my kids. I hoped, I assumed, that they would ultimately benefit from my political activity and respect my life as an activist. It seemed somehow small-minded to put your family first; sort of an extension of putting yourself first. Self. Selfish. I didn't feel that I loved my kids any less because of my commitment to what I thought to be a better future for all.

A good mother would put them first. I should have done everything humanly possible to avoid jail in the first place. Selfish, that was me allowing them to visit and to make the nightmare more real. Would it be any better for Tom to leave them with somebody while he came to see me? I hated to think I still had no idea what was best for my kids. I swore to be a better parent when all this was behind me.

# Chapter 7
# The May Day Rap

In that first group cell, each day was the same nightmare. My nose wrinkled, a nervous tick. Not having any idea about when I was transferring to prison in Gatesville was tormenting. The prospect was always looming on the horizon. It added another layer to my angst and I worried it would topple me. I scrunched my nose some more.

My daily visits from the outside world defined my days. In those fifteen minutes, I was not alone.

It was not enough. I was disconnected. I was alienated. I was desperate to relate to my cellmates. Pat was a bond, but I was trying not to hang on to her like a frightened toddler.

One morning I noticed some of the black women sitting close together. Each woman, one behind the other, combing, stroking, and plaiting the hair of the woman in front of her. They created a soothing circle and I wished to be part of it. At just the right moment, Pat appeared.

"You have thick hair. Let me comb it for you," Pat said.

"When I was little, my mom used to comb my hair and put it in a ponytail and I would always scream. Oh, I'm sorry, I promise I won't scream."

"That's OK. I will be gentle."

And she was. Pat had a large Afro comb. She started from my forehead, down my scalp through my coarse hair. Each stroke more pacifying than the one before. While she untangled my hair with broad strokes of the comb, my neck and shoulders relaxed. My nose stopped wrinkling up and my eyes stopped blinking. Pat was my soul mate. Jail had made us sisters. Tranquility spread down my head through my limbs. Then it dawned on me. Pat took to me precisely because I wasn't her soul mate but a lost soul.

The quiet during the grooming ritual came to an end when a new inmate entered the cell shouting. Blasts, Black Beauties, Bones, Buds, Boomers, Brown Sugar. Do the nasty, Boinking, Wild Thing, Gang Banging, Home Boy wannabe. Fucking A, just gag me with a spoon before I start shitting bricks. It was a different language that reflected a culture that I did not share. It wasn't as if I was a prude, but mastering the new vocabulary would sound fake. Or maybe not. I wasn't that pathetic. Pat had restored something in me, lost soul or not. I could find my soul in rap, fold my arms across my chest and belt out:

> All you scumbags gather round,
> The words you hear be true and sound.
> The pimps in power put me away,
> 'Cusin me of taggin' "May Day."
> Let this be a lesson learned,
> I was caught, unconcerned.
> If you mess with the Red, White, and Blue,
> The heat will surely come down on you.

Those words never left my mouth even if I thought they would be greeted with a laugh at the worst. I knew these ladies had heard everything, and were not in a position to judge anyone. Yet explaining why I got jail time for spray painting had me on the defensive. Not the spray painting as much as the content—the spitting on the flag part. It was meant to be inflammatory. That was the weapon of choice for the RCP. There was still something about controversy that I was attracted to. I just didn't want to be the subject of it.

I didn't write the slogan, so how could I be held responsible? Not that it mattered. Everyone in jail is innocent. I wouldn't have to convince anyone of my innocence, but I would have to explain my past. That would make me look like a weirdo. Or maybe I should have more confidence in my jail-mates. They were the masses after all. Their crimes grew out of poverty, dysfunction, not evil.

It was still another world, as much as I thought I understood it. It was easier dealing with the masses in the abstract, or hawking the *Revolutionary Worker* newspaper, than sharing space with the flesh and blood women twenty-four hours a day in the same close quarters. I wondered whether I could ever fit in with the people on the inside or whether it would be the occasional Pat.

# Chapter 8
# From Limbo to Lean On

Fitting in and being in limbo were not always at odds. Early 1982, following my conviction and a short stint at Bennigan's Restaurant, I went to work at Texas Art Supply. My coworkers were artists, writers, actors, and lost proletariats like me, in different stages of figuring out and establishing our identities. I trusted my coworkers with my past and they included me in their exploration and participation in Houston's flourishing creative scene. Gallery openings every Friday night with free wine!

James Surls ran the newly established Lawndale Center at the University of Houston. Burt Long was a burly African American artist who used a chainsaw to sculpt giant ice blocks into temporal artworks. Falling in with artists allowed me entrance to the alternative art scene in Houston. My friends at Texas Art were involved with Diverse Works, a multidisciplinary performance and art space founded in 1982. This artist space, along with Lawndale Art and Performance Center, propelled Houston beyond the established art world.

When reality hit and I was summoned to jail, my coworkers sprang into action.

Jack, Beth, and Kelly were the core of the Justice for Betty Sullivan Committee. The three of them had an extraordinary friendship that went beyond the confines of Texas Art Supply. They were all artists, with varied experiences.

Jack was the leader. Everyone knew this, even if he wouldn't admit it. It was part of Jack's being to stand up for people who needed help and to protest wrongs. In high school he was drawn to activism. Concern for social issues were as much a part of him as his artwork. I wasn't aware how much so until I was sent off to jail. As Jack said to me:

"The issue was severe injustice, phony set-up, by a secret police system operating out of control, and rubber stamped by an angry judge. A very frightening thing. I said, 'If this can happen to Betty, it can happen to you.' That was my mantra. And it no doubt has happened to countless others, as we now know with other means of forensic testing that eyewitnesses are notoriously wrong.

"And so, to me, even if you were guilty of spray painting, it was wrong because they trumped up the charge to a felony on purpose. The way they showed the photos and pushed the witness towards you as the perp was overt and horrific. I hate bullies of any type, injustice towards those with less power—and this was injustice bully squared. No compassion, no justice.

"I felt much emotion about your dilemma, your incarceration, not the least of which anger and sadness. But I tried not to dwell on that side too much. And also urge others not to. Action instead!"

Jack, Kelly, and Beth contacted radio stations, as well as the *Houston Post* and the *Houston Chronicle*. Jack found a young reporter, Wendy Riss, who would be pivotal in legitimizing my case. If it weren't for Jack, the Justice for Betty Sullivan Committee, and Wendy Riss, my imprisonment would have been a private nightmare.

Other Texas Art Supply coworkers, friends like Josie, departed comrades that Tom and I still were in touch with, and Tom's coworkers all came to my aid. They went above and beyond anyone's idea of friendship. I wasn't expecting that kind of support from friends. My activism came from a commitment to a cause, not a person.

# Chapter 9
# Freak or Fit

Tuesdays and Thursdays were the days everyone with money in their inmate account made out their commissary lists. Wednesdays and Fridays we got our goods. Turning in our lists as well as taking in our booty were high points in the day. From the jail perspective, the thought of grocery shopping, which had been drudgery in my ordinary life, was comparable to a trip to Disneyland.

Commissary was stocked with shampoo, deodorant, paper, pens, and stamps, but the main purchases were junk food, cigarettes, and makeup. Sharing was common, and several women offered me an array of chips, candy, and smokes. The money that Tom sent hadn't worked its way through the channels to appear on my account. Pat's family started a commissary account for her the day she was put behind bars, so that she would have resources until they could make bond. They knew the score. It was comforting to rationalize that my level of anxiety was higher than hers not just because of what I perceived as weaknesses, but because of inexperience. I was only learning the melody; she had the four-part harmony down.

Pat was the calm center to my storm. That was one of the reasons I attached to her. She was resigned to her situation in a good way, like those Chinese finger traps, where the urge to pull your fingers free only tightens the grip of the bamboo cylinder. You relax your fingers and they effortlessly pull away. Pat was my Buddha. Except for the junk food and cigarettes.

After receiving her purchases from commissary, she approached me.

"Want any Fritos or Marlboros? I have plenty."

"Oh, Pat, you don't have to share. I know money is tight."

"There you go again. I'm not too poor to share. And really, I don't need all this."

Another dilemma. The fact was, I never craved salty food and I had once smoked and it was hell getting over that addiction. Now if she offered me some chocolate-that would be tempting. I usually considered only dark chocolate worth the calories, but I could compromise being in jail. I hated to be seen as some kind of health nut instead of one of the regular folks. Compromises, compromises. My values or fit in.

"Thanks, but I'm just not into Fritos. And cigarettes, I'd have a coughing fit. You always share and I don't know how I would survive without you."

"I wish I had the willpower you have. You'd survive without me. You just don't know how strong you are," Pat said.

"You think I'm strong?"

"Of course you are. You have the sense to hang out with me. You aren't pretending to be brave. Only cowards do that."

"That's one way to look at it. I think you'd say something positive in any situation."

"What's wrong with that?"

"Nothing at all."

Pat could have written *Chicken Soup for the Convicts Soul.*

"You know, Pat, all the ladies wear make-up, and maybe I'll buy some. The money will show up in my account soon. It's just slow because of the holidays. I'll splurge on mascara, lipstick, and blush, and put some on for my visits."

"That's the spirit," she said.

Not one to wear much makeup, I heard much later from my friends that I looked like a clown when they saw me at visits. But I fit in better with my cellmates, or at least I presumed to.

Monday, Wednesday, and Friday afternoons, the guards escorted the ladies from my cellblock up to the roof. The minute we reached the top of the stairs and the door opened, most of my cellmates lit up, while I headed for the barbed-wire perimeter of the roof. Smoggy, thick air with the faint whiff of exhaust fumes rose up my nostrils. As women chatted and inhaled nicotine, I pumped my arms and jogged round and round in large loops. I couldn't help myself. Or rather this was one way I could help myself.

Stares that said "crazy lady" washed over me, but my need to work my lungs and legs overruled my self-consciousness. This was one thing I did for myself without any second thoughts. I was always riding a bike as a kid and I played sports in high school. The stress from being inactive and confined to the cell bubbled up like a slow boil, and I needed that release valve of physical activity. Despite the gritty rooftop "track" and the stray woman who crossed my path, my body felt satisfied. Exercising held me whole, if only briefly.

One day, after jogging round and round, Pat looked over at me, flung her half-finished cigarette to the ground, stomped out the butt, and joined in. I was elated.

# Chapter 10
# Meditation

*December 5, 1985*
*Love,*

*Each day is a struggle. One by one by one. So disappointed not to find another letter in the mailbox today. I have re-read the first one four to five times now.*

*You are living in abstract land, deprived of the world, trying to stay grounded, keep cool, and not be bitter. I am in concrete world, swamped with life in all its detail, trying to keep uplifted, stay energetic, and not be bitter. Tony is in who-knows-what-land hoping the nightmare will go away and that the one who brought him into the world will return to help him get into adulthood and not be bitter. Peter is just surviving.*

*I am sustaining momentum from the Shambala weekend. I am sitting about two hours a night average. I do this by cutting out of work on time and flopping down fully clothed as soon as I get home. More naptime, more energy. I usually sit from 10:00 p.m. until 12:00 midnight after the kids are in bed. I tell you, sweets, some kind of power is coming to me. I have felt it fairly intensely this week. I am seeing clearly and precisely and radiating healthiness. All kinds of respect I'm getting. "Getting," ICK! I'm not "getting" anything, but people are sending it my way.*

*Kids and I went out to Brisket House tonight before basketball practice. It is almost a tradition now. Tony and I had chef's salads and Pete a ham sandwich and chocolate pudding for dessert (thinking about you). As you can see, I'm not being too austere with the kids.*

*Sleep calls. Know that you are never alone my dear. We love you very, very much. TB*

When I found a home at Texas Art Supply, Tom went to work for Whole Foods Market. They opened their first store in Houston on Shepherd Street in 1984. The alternative types who didn't work at Texas Art Supply discovered Whole Foods to be an accepting employer. The Creative Writing Program at the University of Houston, founded and led by Donald Barthelme, was in high gear. Several of the graduate students or their significant others found part-time work at Whole Foods and befriended Tom. It was a place, like Texas Art Supply, where you could be yourself.

About the same time, American Tibetan Buddhist practitioners established a local community in Houston. They became, along with his Whole Food friends, invaluable support for Tom.

When Tom first started sitting meditation, I tried too. Sitting crossed-legged on a cushion, my back hurt, my neck cramped, my mind wandered, and my foot fell asleep. It made me nervous, not calm. Or maybe the point was not to be calm but to work through that incessant loop in my head. I wanted to be positive about meditation, but the more I tried, the harder it was. What was grueling for me attracted Tom. He found something, some direction.

At some level I understood that Buddhism was about suffering. Meditation helped its adherents see the world in a more compassionate way, allowing them to break from the categorizations that divide people from one another. The concepts of us, them, self, and others would melt through meditation. Or maybe merge. A clearing, not a nothingness. It sounded good.

But I could never get past the pain and boredom. The sense to delve deep into some place within myself to get out of myself was foreign and frightful. It was a direction I wasn't drawn to. The only reason I tried it in the first place was because Tom did it. I reasoned that if I did embrace meditation, I would be doing it for the wrong reason. That was too close to my personal history. Follow the guy. Just as well that meditation had no appeal. It was better that this was something we would not share. We would find our own paths! Tom was merely ahead of me.

When I went to jail, Tom spent hours sitting on a cushion. I could not comprehend how he did it. What I did comprehend was that he needed meditation to take care of himself, to take care of the kids, to take care of me. Whatever distance and worry it caused me was another thing. It was another anxiety to bury. I needed him to preserve himself, to preserve us all.

Part 2

# Chapter 11
# Gerbil World

**December 3, 1985.**

Late Monday morning, after a lunch I didn't eat, a guard walked through the dorm, approached my bunk, and announced, "Betty, you're getting transferred to a new cell. Here's a pillowcase to put your belongings in. I'll be back soon to take you there."

In under a minute, I stuffed my comb, toothbrush, toothpaste, razor, deodorant, mascara, blush, paper and pen in the pillowcase. I had a few tampons left in a box that I dumped in there too, and I used the container to hold my precious collection of letters. Finished with my packing, I leaped off the bed and searched for Pat, who was sitting at the other end of the dorm in her usual pose, cross-legged on the floor.

"Wow," she said. "What's gotten into you?

"A guard told me I'm being transferred to a new cell. She gave me a pillowcase to pack everything in. Oh my God, it won't be worse than this, do ya think?"

"Calm down. It's funny that you have a pillowcase, since we don't have any pillows. Another great jail mystery. But no, I don't think anything could be worse than this madhouse."

"That's a relief. Oh, Pat, you've been so kind, I can't tell you how much you have helped me. I don't know that I'll ever find someone like you again."

"I'll miss you too. Honestly. I'm nothing special. There are ladies like me all over jail. Anyways I should be getting out myself. Any day now."

This had been Pat's refrain since the moment I met her.

"I know you will," I said and gave her my most confident smile.

"You will be fine. Just keep up that fast walking and the days will fly by."

I squeezed Pat in a hug, then waited for the guard, my arms wrapped around the pillowcase. Two-and-a-half weeks had gone by and it hadn't gotten any worse. Nobody mentioned going to Gatesville prison, so it seemed far away. My friends on the outside were trying to find some angle to keep me out of prison—something about shock probation, someone had a contact with a lawyer that knew Judge Walker. It was out of my hands. My nose was still screwed up, creating wrinkles above my lip, but my head was still attached to my body.

The guard came back and led me out the cell door. We walked past cellblock after cellblock and into an elevator. It rumbled up several stories and delivered us out to another drab hallway. Steel bars lined the halls—bars for walls, bars for doors. If there were windows, there would be bars there too. With every twist and turn, my excitement at leaving the last dorm dampened. I felt like a gerbil in a maze.

At last we arrived at my new cellblock. The guard unlocked the wide cage door, it grinded open, and I was shuffled in. I sniffed around, my imaginary whiskers twitching. Despite the racial mix, the four ladies staring up at the TV all looked the same in their identical faded jail dresses and blank expressions. My arrival was greeted with a series of synchronized nods. Then everyone shifted their gaze back to *All My Children*.

My new cell held only eight women. The rectangle cellblock had a specific layout, not a hodgepodge of bunks surrounded by mattresses. There was a dayroom down the middle, serving as a common area and dining area. It contained two round, metal tables with four matching chairs. Everything was bolted to the floor. The TV hung from the far wall in the back of the room, the one constant in jail interior design.

One of the woman watching TV turned to me and pointed to an open door with, of course, bars. It was one of four individual cells facing an identical four on the long side walls of the dayroom.

I walked into the empty cell. Like Russian dolls, this cell was nested within the bigger group cell, nested within the giant cell they call jail. When I thought about all the bars between me and my family, me and my friends, me and the outside world, it brought a bitter bile taste to my mouth, as if the bars themselves were stuck in my throat.

Shaking those images off, I turned my attention to my new surroundings. Looked at a certain way, there was security. It was my personal gerbil cage. It was a luxury to have a space of my own. I walked over to the metal single bed and sat on the mattress. It had no spring. But at the foot of the bed, there were sheets, a blanket, and a pillow. Aha, now I had use for a pillowcase. I took my hygiene supplies out and meticulously lined up and realigned them on the only shelf in the cell, on the far wall—far being a relative term—too far for my tampon box of letters. I wanted them close by the bed where I would spend most of my time. There was nowhere to put them but on the floor. Not exactly a place of honor, but within reach. All moved in, I went back out to the dayroom to explore.

A payphone was situated near the front of the cell. Eight women shared a phone instead of five-times that. The undertow I felt pulling me down in the old cell was losing its grip. The two toilets and sole shower faced front-out towards the guard-patrolled walkway, as in the previous large cell. The peeing in public would continue. It hadn't become normal, but as nothing was normal in jail, it became another thing to endure and compartmentalize.

In the large dorm the first time I sat on the toilet in full view of other inmates and the guards, I shut my eyes tight. I repeated to myself, "Who cares, nobody's looking, and nobody cares." It became a mantra. And nobody was looking and nobody cared and it was the natural state for a nobody, which is everybody in jail.

The no-privacy policy was to prevent illegal activities. I wasn't sure whether this meant between the inmates, the guards and inmates, or what. We never had physical contact with anyone on the outside. What illegal behavior would I do on the toilet or in the shower that I couldn't do in my own cell under a blanket in bed? There could easily be drama all around me I never detected. Lacking street smarts, I wasn't a keen observer about those sorts of things. Or perhaps the lack of privacy was another way to remove personhood. Our sack-like dresses and flip flops were identical. Our lives were regimented. Our identity was inmate. What was privacy but an acknowledgement of the individual?

As a former communist I hadn't thought individual stuff mattered. How do you have meaningful groups without individuals? I was beginning to think all that oneness had a negative side. We needed both. I needed both.

The few women who hung around the dayroom were still watching TV. The others were in their cells. It didn't seem like prime time to make friends, so I went back into my cell. I wondered if I'd find another Pat. As selfish as it was, I was happy that she hadn't gotten bailed out before I was moved. It's not like I willed it that way, so I didn't feel entirely guilty. I just didn't believe I could last in that hellhole without clinging to her. With the transfer to the smaller cell, I felt less desperate. It was rather peaceful. No shouting. At some point I'd strike up a conversation without appearing needy. I could get my act together. Tomorrow.

That night there was an announcement over the intercom. "Cell doors will be shutting in ten minutes. Get ready for bed." A small line formed at the toilets, after which everyone disappeared into their cells. The lights in the cellblock dimmed and the door to my cell growled shut. It was neither dark nor light. I lay down on my mattress and looked up at the ceiling. I clutched my letter box like a stuffed animal and sang to myself, "The first days are the hardest days, don't you worry, don't you know, dah, dah, dah, dah, dah . . ." a line I half-remembered from the Grateful Dead. The song played and played in my head. Identifying with my gerbil pets at home, enclosed but alive, I resolved to make tomorrow a better day. I could connect with Pat. I could connect with the other ladies. We were all little caged rodents. We were in this together. We needed to bond to survive.

The next day started at 4:30 a.m. with the alarm clock of metal on metal clanking as the eight cell doors opened simultaneously for breakfast. In the first dorm, I regularly missed breakfast. The times I tried to negotiate my way down from the top bunk, I'd hit the same spot on my shin and the bruise on my leg reminded me that getting onto the floor half-asleep wasn't worth the effort.

With the single bed, breakfast wasn't entirely off limits. Plus I vowed to meet my new neighbors. I took cautious steps out of my cell, ensuring I'd be last. One of the tables had an empty spot, where I sat. The breakfast trays were already set up. Nestled among the rock-hard biscuit, gravy slop, sticky, gooey oatmeal, was a beaming orange.

I turned to the woman sitting next to me. "This orange looks great. I haven't seen a piece of fresh fruit in what seems like forever."

"Don't get your hopes up. We don't get them regular. Sometimes we get a hardboiled egg instead of that powdered shit. That's the only reason I even get up for breakfast," she said.

"Hardboiled egg? I'd get up for that too. Have you been here long?" I asked.

"A couple of weeks. I have a three-month sentence. How long is yours?

"Two years. I'm supposed to go to Gatesville," I said.

"Pullin' chain?"

"Pull in what?"

"You must be new to all this. My name is Bobbie. Pullin' chain is what they call it when you get transferred to Gatesville. Every Wednesday, in the middle of the night, well about 2:00 a.m. Thursday, which is still the middle of the night in my book, they round up the ladies with prison sentences, put them on a bus, and off they go. There's no warning. Wednesday night, all the ladies waiting to pull chain get jittery. You'll see."

"That sounds horrible. Why don't they give any warning?"

"I guess they don't want the bus to be ambushed or nothin' like that. Who knows if there is a reason or not? Those folks could be just messing with our minds."

"I guess so. Thanks, Bobbie, I'm glad you warned me about pullin' chain and glad to know I'm not the only one who wonders why things happen the way they do around here."

Bobbie, with her high cheekbones, long neck, and light brown skin, looked like she could have been a model from some exotic country, except for the scar that extended from the side of her nose past her mouth and down her neck. Not to mention the crude cross tattoo on her forearm. She was from Louisiana, Creole, where a mixture of Black, Native American, and French was not unusual.

I peeled the skin off the orange and held it up to my nose. At that moment nothing in the world could have smelled better than that pungent aroma. I loved fruit, but oranges were one of those overly ordinary winter offerings that only found their way into my grocery cart when Texas ruby red grapefruit was not available. I would never be an orange snob again. I drew the orange up to my mouth to take a luxurious bite.

This time Bobbie turned towards me with her eyes squinting.

"You really going to Gatesville?"

"Yeah, it's crazy. I got convicted for spray painting, and since I was a radical—well, a communist at the time—I know I definitely got screwed." There, let it all hang out.

"What! I don't know anything about communism but going to Gatesville for spray painting, that makes no sense. You sure you didn't knock off someone in the process?"

"I didn't even do the spray painting. It was the Exxon building that got painted and it was an anti-American slogan, so some folks got offended."

"Honey, it doesn't matter if you did it or not, just if you could have. As for me, I'm the rare breed that admits to being an addict and a crook. But that's all gonna change. I'm going to AA when I get out of here. Been saying that for a long time, but I can't take another bust. And I swear it will be the change I need."

"I've heard great things about AA. We all need help, and asking for it is the first step, they say," I said, dispensing wisdom *a la* Pat.

"That's the truth."

I drank a few sips of muddy coffee. Bobbie and the others started getting up and going back into their cells, and I followed. This was the drill, back to bed after breakfast at whatever time it was. I only knew breakfast was at 4:30 a.m. because I was told ahead of time. It could be any time. Was not knowing the time mind-control too?

At 7:00 a.m. the intercom came on again: "Get ready for head count, ladies." I woke up from my half-sleep and peeked out of my cell. The personal cell doors stayed opened between breakfast and bedtime. The ladies lined up outside their cells, not quite at attention. I scrambled up and stood with my hand over my face suppressing a yawn. The main cell door opened and a guard showed up in the common area for the head count.

She walked down one side of the cellblock and up the other counting 1, 2, 3, 4, 5, 6, 7, 8.

"All accounted for," she shouted. As if there was any place we could possibly go. Before leaving, the guard turned on the TV as most of us shuffled back into our cells again. There were a few hardcore TV aficionados who watched *Good Morning America*.

Like most of the others, I lay around in bed until 10:30 a.m., even if I wasn't sleeping, just to make the day go by. 10:30 was lunchtime. It was never appealing, not to mention the early hour. At the most I ate the dessert washed down with the sweetest Kool Aid.

In the early afternoons I parked myself in the dayroom. The TV was a constant. I wished soap operas didn't repulse me. For the ladies it was a second family, and watching them make catty comments brought them together as jail-family too. There was no way to be part of one family without being part of the other. I had to find a way to suck it up.

So I forced myself to watch TV. I met Janice who didn't write hot checks, Leyla who didn't shoot up, Kim who didn't shoplift, Marcelina who didn't stab her boyfriend, Caron and Darla who didn't talk about it. On *General Hospital* there was Ginger who nearly died from a late term abortion, Tina who was having an affair with her stepfather, and Andrea who disappeared. I realized that the soaps dealt with the same problems my cellmates had, only in a more glamorous lifestyle.

Watching TV made more sense. It wasn't wasting time; it made the time go by. I could do this, at least some of the time. I was hanging out, but it still felt like I was faking it.

Fortunately recreation was still three days a week. Unlike the situation in the first big dorm, all the ladies from my cellblock were eager to venture out. The first time we lined up to be herded up to the roof, I was surprised to hear the rare sound of giggling. Either for exercise or smoking, these women must value fresh air! There seemed to be a level of anticipation I hadn't sensed in my old dorm cell. As we were led into the hallway and waited by a freight-sized elevator, a procession of male prisoners walked by. They were steered to the far wall from us and told not to move as we were hustled along, hugging the other wall. A chorus of catcalls rang out from the men. The women from my cell whistled and hooted back. A shot of current surged through the line of women. Men, in the flesh, not behind Plexiglas. The hair on my arms stood up. They were wearing orange jumpsuits. Some had their short sleeves rolled up, showing off muscular biceps. Our convict brothers. It was immediate attraction. I didn't expect these men's crude expressions to feel like compliments. But they did. We were still desirable. We drew another living being's attention. It was totally flattering.

This was so different than anything I'd experienced. My previous attitude would be to feel insulted and disgusted. When I lived in New York and the occasional construction worker whistled at me as I walked down the street, I'd shoot the finger at them.

Just like an orange or hardboiled egg showing up on the breakfast tray, it was reason enough for all the women in my cellblock to make the trip to the barren rooftop for recreation. It was more than reason; it was hope.

I was devoted to exercising. My contracting leg muscles and pounding heart were what I needed to feel alive. Seeing the men became an added bonus. Not that I participated in the whooping exchanges. And I certainly didn't put on makeup before our rooftop excursions, like most of my cellmates.

If no men to talk about were seen on the way to recreation, my fast-walking became a secondary diversion. Who would join me? I was proud to have company from different women. I imagined myself the fitness Mama, as Mama was a common term for any inmate over thirty. Bobbie was my most consistent partner. She was speedy herself so I didn't have to slow down even when we talked. That was another plus. Walking led to talking.

"I think all the time about the people I hurt with my drinking and drugging," she said as we rounded the parameter of the roof. "I heard in AA they tell you to apologize, but bad as I feel I can't see that I have the nerve to apologize. Have you done much apologizing?"

"Not really. I've thought a lot about it. I know that's not enough. It's hard for me, too."

I wanted to apologize to my mother. She got cancer and died in her early sixties. She lived in New York and I was in Texas. She had surgery and went through chemo while I was separating from my first husband, Joe.

I couldn't even say what went wrong with me and Joe, although it was a wrenching time. We were both devoted communists, so you would think that our emotional bond was strong. But emotions were something we didn't pay attention to. I had no language for my needs. Or awareness.

My mother's decline was in another orbit. I didn't take in how serious my mother's condition was. I wasn't paying attention to what she was going through. I went up to visit with my kids a month before she died. It didn't sink in how bad she was until I got there and saw her frail body. I've always felt terrible about all that. It was not something I could make up for.

It would be easy to blame ideology for everything. My role as a communist so dominated my personal self and relationships. But I think I never was one to be tuned in to other people. I could have been more conscious and responsive to what was going on with my mom, communist or not.

"I think we all hurt people we love, without thinking," Bobbie said. "They say you have to forgive yourself first."

"I've heard that, too. I don't know how to do that."

"I don't know, either. That's why I read my bible. Making up for lost time when my grandma tried to get me to go with her to church and I always managed to run away."

Forgiveness was foreign, but guilt was right at home. I remembered something I attributed to Woody Allen along the lines of, "If we didn't have guilt, we wouldn't know how to act right." If embracing guilt was a way of taking responsibility for my choices, I could do that. Maybe guilt was a stage in the process. First awareness, then guilt, then forgiveness?

And my kids—there was plenty of guilt I felt about them. But I could do something about that! Only thing was I had to wait until after supper, which was when I regularly called home.

The time crawled by. I couldn't read, I couldn't write. TV was starting to make me depressed. Then I remembered that Kelly sent Xeroxed pictures of yoga poses along in a letter. Yoga seemed a little too close to meditation for me, but it was worth a try. I sat on my cell floor bending my arms over my outstretched legs. They didn't reach very far. Kelly wrote, "Remember, out with the red air, in with the blue." I hoped I was filling myself with good air and getting rid of bad air. I forced myself to continue doing yoga and breathing. The breathing was calming: in through my nose, out through my mouth.

The cell doors were opened and dinner trays deposited in the dayroom. The food was barely edible, which was fine. I was in a hurry to call home.

After the supper trays were taken away, I was first in line to use the phone. I calculated it was around 5:00 p.m., the time when everyone was home and expected my daily phone call.

I picked up the receiver on the pay phone and dialed "O" for operator. All calls were collect, including local ones. The operator came on the line and asked whomever said hello, "Collect call from Betty Sullivan, will you accept the charges?"

Tony answered as he usually did, accepted the charges, and said, "Hi, Mom."

I gushed, "Hi, sweetheart, how is your day going? You know I love you and miss you so much. I'm so proud of you. Do you know that?"

"Yes, Mom. Are you OK?"

"Yes, sorry, just been thinking a lot about you kids. How is school?"

"School's OK. I've been organizing my baseball cards."

"Wow, that's great, how many do you have now?"

"I'm not sure, but the bottom drawer of my dresser is full."

"Sounds wonderful. I bet you know all the names and teams."

"I don't know all the names, but I do know a lot. Do you want to talk to Pete?"

"Sure, you know I love you and miss you so much, Tony."

"Yes, I know."

"Peter," I'd say when he came on the phone. "I love you and miss you so much. How is school?"

"It's fine, Mommy."

"Have you been playing basketball?"

"Yes, my team won its first game."

"That's so wonderful. You are such a good basketball player."

"Maybe."

"You know I love you and miss you so much."

I wondered if I sounded like a robot. I didn't know how else to express how much I loved them and missed them, other than repeating it over and over. I hoped that it stayed with them after the phone call. For me, hearing the word "Mom" from Tony and "Mommy" from Pete was all I needed. I'd always be their mother. They would always be my sons.

Tom got on the line last. He said Tony and Pete were still spending most weekends with Joe and Gail as usual. All the parents seemed confident that the kids were safe, despite Joe and Gail's continuing concern about FBI surveillance.

Tom and I discussed Tony's options for middle school the next year. We were looking for a magnet program that he had to apply for in the spring. Tom was in the process of getting all the needed paperwork together for applications. Tom would send me copies and more information in the mail. The phone call reassured me that we were still together as a family.

I often called friends in Houston, too. I felt like a ghost lurking around other people's lives, but everyone I spoke to said it meant a lot to them to hear my voice and know that I was OK. I wondered if they were humoring me, like telling a sick person they look just great. It was hard to comprehend the outpouring of heart when I felt like baggage.

# Chapter 12
# Dad

Fridays and Saturdays the lights in the common area of the cell stayed on and the doors to our personal cells stayed open until 1:30 a.m. Fortunately the sound on the TV was turned down and the intercom was quiet. A few of my cellmates stayed up watching late-night talk shows, but not many. Those weekend nights I didn't feel pressured to take part in group TV consuming and retreated to my cell with anticipation. The extra light illuminating from the dayroom created a kind of twilight zone. It was a time to indulge in my own illicit activities.

Before tucking myself into bed, I unfolded a thin napkin that revealed a piece of white bread scavenged from lunch. I finger-scooped a dab of peanut butter from a small jar of Skippy's, bought from the commissary, and smeared it on the bread. Saving anything from a meal to eat later was considered contraband, as we were told it would attract insects. That made sense until I thought about the half-eaten candy bars and bags of chips that were all over the place. Rescuing a piece of bread from lunch for a midnight snack was doing no harm. There were only so many rules I was going to follow, and this wasn't one of them.

With my peanut butter nosh assembled, I unearthed my most illegal item packed at the bottom of my tampon letter box, a deck of hand-crafted playing cards.

Playing cards were not available through the commissary, as they would "encourage gambling." I made my own by saving up paper napkins from meals and tearing them into rectangles until there were fifty-two neat ones. Using a pencil to write readable numbers on the napkins without tearing them is harder than you may think, and playing with floppy cards had its challenges. To shuffle I gently scattered the upside-down cards on my blanket and randomly reconstructed them back into a pile. Sunday through Thursday my cards stayed hidden. Weekend nights I threw my own private party and played solitaire. Not entirely private. My dad was with me. He shared so much of himself when I was incarcerated that it transformed our relationship. My dad loved to play cards, and I was channeling him.

My father played a card game called klaberjass, which is similar to pinochle. He learned it growing up on the Lower East Side of New York City. A Hungarian shop-owner drew in young men to play cards and gamble on folding chairs set up outside his store. My father, quick with math, picked up the game easily. He played this game throughout his life, with or without the exchange of money, first with the regulars in his old neighborhood, then in the army. My dad continued the tradition in Roslyn Heights with friends who had similarly migrated from the tenements of New York City to the suburbs after World War II. Dad taught the game to anyone who would let him—that anyone being a male.

It fascinated me to watch my father and his buddies on weekend nights, with their scotch on the rocks and cigars, sit around a table playing this game without exchanging a word. They would knock once or twice on the card table and throw out or pick up cards. There was no cash exchanged, but they kept score. The workings of the game were a mystery to me. It came from a different time and place. While the men played cards, my mother and the other wives hung out in the kitchen, chatting away. When no fellow card players were around, my dad played solitaire. That he did teach me. From then on playing solitaire conjured up images of my father.

He was a real character, not only the dominant figure in my family, but the patriarch of the extended Baer clan. My dad worked for the IRS and was always good with money, but counter to the Jewish stereotype, he was unquestionably generous, especially when it came to family.

One evening my mother was clanking around in the kitchen preparing supper when Dad arrived home from work. I was in my room listening to the radio and heard my new favorite song. I burst into the kitchen and said, "I've got to get '*A Hundred Pounds of Clay!*'" He shot a glance at me. Having no idea I was referring to a song title, he said, "I think I could get that cheaper in the city."

Another day my Dad brought home a live toucan for a pet. We already had our dachshund Lucy, and we named the bird Louie. Louie was quite amusing. He lived in a colossal cage in our paneled den. My brother John and I would let him out to fly around the room and we would throw grapes up in the air, which Louie caught on the wing. We, especially myself, never tired of this sport. My mother objected to having Louie flying around the den because after Louie snapped up the fruit, he expelled a poop. My mom, who had extraordinary hearing and smelling abilities, would always know when we let Louie out of his cage, as careful and quiet as we tried to be. She'd fling open the den door in the middle of our Louie sessions and say:

"Who is going to clean up after this bird?"

"Clean up what?" I'd ask.

"Louie's poop, of course. I know that bird messes up the den every time you let him out of the cage. I heard him flapping around when I was in the kitchen."

John and I looked at each other. Did we really expect to get away with anything?

"Mom, I have to do homework," I'd say.

"I have a test to study for," my brother would say.

"But we can do it later," we chimed in.

My mother would march off to the kitchen, shaking her head. We would get Louie back in his cage and slink away. My mother returned with paper towels and Lysol spray to clean up after Louie, as we knew she would. Interestingly my parents didn't stop us from letting Louie out of his cage. They were the opposite of disciplinarians.

My dad's eccentric tendencies were expressed in other ways. He had a collection of color-splashed bowties that he wore to work every day. He must have had hundreds. Monday to Friday my dad commuted to work in Manhattan on the Long Island Rail Road, adorned in his flashy bowtie reading *The New York Times*, folded like origami. My brother and mother read the newspaper too, but my mom read mostly *Newsday*, the Long Island paper, her sharp eyes scrutinizing the sale ads.

That's one reason I was elated the day the *Houston Post* showed up at jail. It was another link to my family. How a newspaper found its way to our dayroom regularly was another enigma. Who cared? I devoured it. It wasn't only my world growing up where newspapers were revered, Joe and Tom were avid readers and started the day reading the paper. This was a good influence on Tony and Pete, who became newspaper lovers too, even if they all checked out the sports page first. Except for my father, his focus was the business section.

Reminiscing about my dad wouldn't have amounted to that much if wasn't for the daily contact we had through letters. As sure as I had a visit every day, I'd get a letter in the mail from my dad every night—literally every single night. I'd write him back in time for the mail to be picked up the next day. Every day. Our letters stayed in sync through my entire incarceration.

Dad shared his experiences in the 29th Infantry during WWII. When we were growing up, the only thing he related to his war experience was that he would not allow our family to picnic. He stated more than once, "I will never eat off the ground again."

*Dec. 8, 1985*
*My Dear Daughter, Betty,*

*To continue the saga of my short but memorable experience in the army, the way to keep clean and warm in the open or in the cellars of France and Germany is as follows:*

*I wore seven rather heavy undershirts and an outer wool shirt. I looked like a barrel from my neck to my waist. I would take off all the seven tops, take a bird bath, then take the top that was closest to my body and make that the outer layer next to my shirt. In this way I had a clean one for a week or so.*

*When we were in a rest area, I would take off the three or four top ones and send it to the laundry. I would fill up my helmet with water, removing the helmet liner, and brush my teeth. I would spit out the water and with a rag and a small piece of soap I kept in my pocket, would wash my face and neck and wrists. I shaved after I brushed my teeth. The water was not dumped. Then I would wash my armpits. The crotch was next and finally my ankles and toes. When the water was finished, it was dark and dirty. The water was about two-and-a-half quarts. The job of taking off seven undershirts exercised my arms. I did lose a great deal of weight (I must have been one-hundred-fifteen pounds) as I was too tired to eat, and I lived on Me D bars (chocolate) for three days. The long johns were size twenty and it was necessary for me to pin them up. The food in the rest area was barely edible and when I was sent to the hospital sometime in April, I could barely stand.*

*When the war was over in Europe and the war in the Pacific was still on, the men from the 29th Infantry Division were given a physical exam for possible deployment to Japan. I was classified as "C" or unfit for further combat duty. I imagine that if necessary and the need for replacements arose I would have been changed to A or B. Never had a chance to rest up until I was transferred to Morning Reports sometime in September, 1945.*

*The similarity between my overseas combat and your imprisonment have a good deal in common [sic]. I left your mother and John. You are separated from your family. But only for a limited time, as well. It will pass, as mine did. The family and friends who love you can have compassion, but only those who have had the experience could feel as you have felt: the hunger for husband and children and, I may add, father. This too will pass. You can be sure that your experience will be absolutely different to explain and no one except your immediate family could or probably would understand. Love, Dad*

# Chapter 13
# Reality?

My days in jail blurred together. To keep track, I X-ed off day after day on my handmade calendar. This act confirmed that time passed no matter what, one comforting truism I could embrace. Instead of "Seizing the Time" or thinking I shouldn't waste precious time, I wanted time to slip away, the faster the better. No one could control time and if anything was on my side, that was it.

The week was defined by the dread of pullin' chain. The words themselves sounded ominous, like Russian roulette. I would hear the click of a revolver and prepare to receive a bullet in the heart. So far there were only blanks. At some point I knew it would get me. I just didn't know when. As I was never certain when I went to bed on Wednesday night whether I would be gone by Thursday morning, I always wrote a letter to Tom (TB, a term of endearment for Tommy Bob) and the kids before going to sleep. Bobbie promised she would mail it for me Thursday morning if I was taken away.

*December 18, 1985*
*Dearest TB*

*I really hope I get to stay here in Harris County as long as possible. To think of spending at least a month without being able to speak to you and the kids, not to mention months of not seeing all of you makes me miserable and it makes me cry. I still feel strong, but it's a melancholy strong. Sometimes when I'm writing other people I don't want to sound too depressed, even if I feel a bit weathered. But I don't want to imply I'm so strong nothing can touch me here, like I'm invincible, because that would be a ridiculous position to assume. I want people to get strength from me as I from them, yet I'm longing to get out of here. That goal is what I'm looking and concentrating all my energy towards.*

*Our love has been the thing that kept me and keeps me going. And I think you and the kids will grow closer through this too. I hate the fact that I'm separated from all of you. It is a struggle not to get depressed and bitter. I feel strong, I feel your strength, but it is not automatic. I'm constantly reaching inside for strength and mindful of all the love from the outside—we are lucky there is so much to draw on. My feelings for you guys are so intense and passionate I seriously think I'm going to burst sometimes . . .*

*You know I get up at 4:30 a.m. so I think of you getting ready for work, it's kind of a private moment seeing you hustling around the house . . . Last night as I went to sleep I imagined myself as a transparent spirit cuddling next to you as you slept . . . I walked to the kids' room and kissed Tony on the top bunk goodnight and Peter on the bottom bunk. You were all sleeping so soundly and beautifully. I was there with you and it made me cry and feel happy at the same time . . . When this is over I'll be there every night with all of you . . .*

Reality?

*Being able to relax my guard and look introspectively? Being in jail and facing the suffering here and yet so much has been kept alive and growing. Transcendence, spiritual wealth, the semantics don't matter. It's part of that less concrete world, yet ever so real.*

*It is hard to relate to, me being so UN-spiritual. I'm quite the pragmatist, it is what it is and all that, but I think there is some sort of spiritual fascia that connects us all—the web of life? . . . When I see you and the kids at visits and everyone looks so calm and serene, so steady and strong, it gives me such fulfillment. I feel enveloped in love and goodness and somehow totally grounded yet oblivious to space and time. Like the time we saw the movie Cocoon and those space creatures made love without touching. It was some incredible exchange of good vibrations. One of those things I'll never understand but don't care because just feeling it is all you need. That's pretty good for me. I usually don't trust things I can't understand intellectually . . .*

*Some people call their cells home, but I never will— my home is in your hearts.*

*I love you all,*
*Betty*

I spent hours in my cell sitting cross-legged on my cot, reading, writing, or going through my box of letters. The gerbil in me warmed up to this place. It kept me in but also kept others out. I felt a strange sense of sanctuary, nestled in my cage. It was all in how I perceived it. I was beginning to wonder if reality was anything more than a subjective perception. I read about how people survived much worse than me by creating a mental place to escape to.

Looking through my letters, I recognized everyone's penmanship—each unique. It was like hearing their voices. My friends would write to me about all sorts of things: funny stories, philosophy, social commentary, poetry. Artists, as many of them were, they added drawings. Mostly, though, they wrote about love.

My family of Tom, Tony, and Pete was the stable one. Many of my friends weren't married, and if they were, they had all sorts of stressors. I felt like Ann Landers. I was the depository of love gone wrong. In another way, my imprisonment gave them a rallying point. In a letter from Kelly, after pages of detail about her boyfriend Ken's move to Dallas, she wrote:

> . . . I had this relationship with Ken for so many years and now that it's over, it feels uneven, unfinished, because I couldn't get him to talk. Yet I know he was becoming unsatisfied and I was also pulling away. But he still wasn't honest about his feelings. I know it is really finally over, because of the distance. We are really separated and each day we grow more independent from each other, less and less in touch, the sad part is, I feel like I'll never meet anyone again who could make me as happy as Ken once did.
>
> I guess that's why seeing you felt so good. I saw the hope and courage you have to get through all the sorrow life hands us, and I felt inspired. I know that may sound a little corny, but it's true.

Along with news of her love life, she went on to say:

*Well enough about my saga, I must catch you up to date on the "Justice for Betty Sullivan Committee." Yes! "Justice for Betty Sullivan" is now being worked into a poster that will have all the pertinent information about you and how people can write their congressman. I'm going to talk to Judge Seals tomorrow about writing a pardon petition for the Governor. Gary Okly is contacting the TV stations. I don't know of any concrete great thing—only that we are doing the best we can in educating the public about this injustice and I think it is working. We are doing everything we can think of and we feel good about it. I want and need to help you in anyway, and so this media campaign is a very positive thing for me and hopefully in the long run for you. You wouldn't believe how concerned people are. It makes me feel good for you instead of sad. I know somehow this energy of concern must get back to you and make you stronger.*

*It is very late now and I have to work tomorrow so I'm going to finish this now. Remember yoga, out with the red air and in with the blue!*

*Call me when you can and thank you for listening. I feel like I'm all cried out in my beer now. Thanks, you're a real pal! I mean that too.*

*I love you—forever, Kelly*

Another time she wrote:

*Betty, I've been looking through the* I Ching *and came across something that entirely sums up how I feel about you and why I care so much!*

*Book 8: Holding Together*
*Holding Together brings good fortune.*
*Inquire of the oracle once again.*
*Whether you possess sublimity, constancy and perseverance;*
*Then there is no blame.*
*Those who are uncertain gradually join.*
*Whoever comes too late*
*Meets with misfortune.*

*The* I Ching *says that what is required is that we unite with others, in order that all may complement and aid one another through holding together. But such a "hold together" calls for a central figure around whom other persons may unite. To become a center of influence, holding people together is a "grave" matter and fraught with great responsibility. It requires greatness of spirit, consistency, and strength. That's you, Betty!*

My friends and family were the source of my strength. It was their greatness of spirit and consistency that was remarkable, not mine. If I could keep wrapped up in those warm and powerful connections, I could transcend the physical world, create my own reality, and survive anything.

# Chapter 14
# Holidays for Whom?

Thanksgiving, Hanukkah, Christmas, and New Years were rough. TV, used like a drug to escape the present, now turned on us like a bad trip. The commercials and shows about happy family gatherings and the latest toys were harrowing. Every ad for cranberry sauce and Nintendo video games piled on another layer of despair.

My kids had loving grandparents and step-grandparents to shelter them. Since we started living together and got married, Tom and I regularly traveled to Oklahoma City with Tony and Pete to visit his parents and siblings who gathered there for Thanksgiving. This year he took them alone.

For Christmas the kids went with their dad and stepmother to Massachusetts, where Joe's parents lived. Fortunately all of our family ties were deep. As much as the extended family didn't understand why we chose to reject our middle-class upbringing and become communists, there was never a doubt that blood was thicker than politics. The arrival of grandkids made those ties stronger. Tony and Pete were the first grandkids for both of our families and easily became the main attractions.

I was not a Christmas person, but Christmas with Joe's family was more of a feel-good family food festival then consumer frenzy with religious overtones. I remembered the mouthwatering mussels with home-cooked Italian biscuits and marinara sauce I had at Christmas years ago when Joe and I were married. I knew Joe's mother would still be cooking her love into those meals and was happy that the kids were doing normal things over the holidays. I hoped that getting away from Houston would clear their minds of my imprisonment. Concentrating on their happiness would pull me through to the New Year.

For Christmas a church group gathered tube socks, shampoo samples, and red pocket combs as gifts for the women inmates. They were packed in red and green Santa Claus bags and passed out by the guards. Jail was not chilly; with all the bodies crowded together, we generated our own heat. But since the only foot-covering we had was flip flops, the tube socks were appreciated. Underneath that appreciation was a nagging feeling I couldn't figure out. Something just didn't sit right. It wasn't resentment. It was more internalized. I was embarrassed.

The church ladies became my benefactors, and I envisioned myself a street urchin. A dirty face with a cap held in my upturned hand, looking for a pittance. I figured the church women's gifts were coming from a good place. I didn't resent them. Even if a little pity was part of their caring, sharing their good fortune with the less fortunate was honorable. I hoped my political involvement didn't come off as doing something for the less fortunate. When I was so involved in political activity, thinking how other people viewed me wasn't part of my orientation. I was doing the right thing. That's all that mattered.

Going to jail and passing out Christmas gifts was generous. It took time and effort. Then why didn't this gesture lift my spirits? Instead it reinforced the essence of the jail experience, dependence and passivity.

While I watched the other inmates line up to get their share of Christmas goodies from the guard, it struck me that as much as I wanted to be accepted by the other women in jail, I was ashamed to be identified with them. Lumped in that category of the needy. I hoped this wasn't pride. I was privileged because of the life I was born into. That shouldn't make me feel like I was better than my cellmates.

I got in line and took my Christmas bag and rationalized that socks were just socks. Maybe my cellmates didn't even care about the socks and were accepting them in the name of good manners. I could have good manners too. There was nothing to be ashamed of.

Most of my cellmates, in fact, wore the socks. They were cozy. It became a winter fashion statement that added levity. The thick, white socks had either red stripes or blue stripes at the calf, as if they designated basketball teams. We even exchanged the socks, as they were one size fits all and some ladies wanted the blues and others the red ones. The socks were the bulkiest piece of clothing we had, and we laughed at the way our socked-over big toe poked out of the flip flop straps as if we had webbed feet. A picture of me in a cotton jail dress with those high socks and awkward footwear was taken for the *Houston Style* article. The tube socks were now part of my public image. I wondered if anyone noticed how strange it looked.

While Tony and Pete were away for the Christmas holidays, Tom had Kent, his best friend growing up in Oklahoma City, who had moved to New York, come for a visit. I had met Kent previously and we had connected over homemade Borscht soup. He was a lone Jew in Oklahoma and moved to the East Coast. The opposite of my journey. Kent was keenly aware that he was a minority and relocating to New York was where he found his people—along with bagel stores and Jewish delis on every corner. Even though I shuddered at being identified with a religion, I couldn't help but feel a kinship towards Jews I met, as few and far between as that was in Texas.

With the kids in Massachusetts, Tom and Kent were headed on a road trip to Austin. Tom was overjoyed to have companionship and get away. Before they left they came to see me in jail.

I was glad Kent wanted to come visit me with Tom. It was important for me to let him know the real deal about jail. Talking on the phone on the other side of the petition in the visiting room, I told him that women were typically arrested for bad checks, drugs, public intoxication, and prostitution. And how jail was such a poor solution to those problems. These women were victims themselves, I stressed. If there were any way to change people's perception on the outside of women on the inside, I would have done something useful. My time incarcerated would help to humanize the stereotype of jailbirds. I don't know whether wanting to get that kind of message out was a continuation of my radical history or a personality trait. Certainly anything close to proselytizing wasn't promoted in Judaism. Wherever it was coming from, I imagined Kent sharing what he did during his vacation . . . "I spent Christmas with my buddy in Houston, and we visited his wife in jail. I saw some of the other inmates talking to visitors and none of them looked menacing. I think we as a society need to tackle the root causes—poverty, addiction, dysfunctional families—of why these women are incarcerated. Yes, there is personal responsibility on their part, but we still need empathy." Then a debate would start about the connection between capitalism and the criminal justice system. I smiled to think I had made a difference, even if I had no idea what, if anything, Kent said when he got home about his visiting me in jail.

As happy as I was that Tom had Kent for support, I couldn't repress a sense of jealousy. It was just a little trip. Tom made sure that other friends covered my visitation schedule even during the busy holidays. Tom deserved some fun in Austin. He could drink margaritas and eat spicy tacos, stay up late going to clubs on 6th street. He could do all those things, and more, with me stuck behind bars.

Everyone in my cell, probably the whole jail, was relieved when the holidays were over. As the barrage of TV commercials filled with Transformers and Cabbage Patch dolls dried up, a collective weight lifted. I hated that tug in my soul. I hated creeping envy that my family was enjoying themselves without me. But I wanted them to share in the distraction and joyful times the holidays could afford.

How easy to see families slipping away and making a life without the pariah of an incarcerated mother. I knew this was far from my reality, but I was close enough to see how this could happen. The women I lived with, not wanting to fade away yet knowing that their very presence was shaming for their families. I shared the mutual sense of being a liability.

Bobbie said, "It's easy to want to imprison the people on the outside. I'm trying so hard not to let my family go. I know it's not right. What if they are better off without me?

# Chapter 15
## It Takes a Village

I was sitting on the bunk in my cell occupied with writing letters when three guards marched into the dayroom. *The Young and the Restless* was blaring on the TV. The women watching weren't restless, so I figured the guards' intrusion was no big deal. I was wrong.

One of the three guards who entered our cell shouted, "In a line, ladies!" The women watching TV jumped to their feet, the others sprung from their cells. I hadn't seen my cellmates move that fast before. I stepped out of my cell, dragging one foot at a time.

"Lift up your dress and spread your cheeks," was the next order.

Each inmate bent over and held her butt cheeks wide. The first guard marched behind the women. One by one, she peered up each asshole. She got to Bobbie and stopped.

"Wider!" the second guard shouted.

Bobbie squeezed her eyes shut as she tugged at her flesh. The guard squatted down behind her as if she was ready to punt a football.

The third guard remained at the main cell door. She barked to the women already searched "Don't you dare straighten back up until we're done with everybody."

I was at the end of the line, wishing I had been at the front. The asshole-checking guard came closer and closer. I could tell there was no physical contact, but my nerves were jangled just the same. A quick surge of what must be adrenaline came over me, yet there were no fight or flight options. Freeze. Is that an adrenaline response too? Shut out this new assault and steel myself. Holding my breath and hardening my body, I bent over, assuming the position.

Where the hell would I get anything to shove up my butt? I held onto this welcome surge of anger. Those motherfuckers.

The guards ended the search. "Nobody go back to your cells yet. Take a seat at the tables."

We scrambled for the chairs and sat down in silence.

One guard stood watch over us and the other two split up and went into our individual cells. They stripped the covers off the beds, throwing the pillows to the floor. They rummaged through our books and papers. They shook our shampoo bottles and rooted around our toothbrushes and makeup. They came out of the cells holding contraband; a leftover biscuit squirreled away from breakfast, an extra blanket taken from an inmate's bed after she left for Gatesville.

Without a word the guards marched out.

All the tension in the room exploded like heat lightning.

"Fuck this shit."

"What a bunch of crap this is."

"Don't those guards have anything better to do than harass us?

"I know this is jail and I don't expect the Hilton, but a little basic dignity would help."

Bobbie chimed in, "I could understand if they were looking for drugs or weapons. But I'm an old lady and just want to serve my time."

"They busted up our cells for stupid stuff like an extra blanket?"

"Wonder what's up their assholes."

The cursing that normally embarrassed me sounded so sweet.

"Yeah, fuck this shit," I repeated.

Bobbie turned to me, clenching her teeth and said, "The guards rack up our cell and search us like that every few weeks in case we forget we're at their mercy."

Most of the women went back to their cells to put things right. There was a broom and dustpan kept near the phone. Bobbie took the broom and started sweeping the dayroom. Something about cleaning eased the tension. My paper-towel playing cards weren't among the contraband the guards waved in our faces as they exited the cell, but I still wanted to make sure they were not disturbed. Yet here was Bobbie, engaged in the collective cleanup. I stopped short from entering my cell.

"Hey, I can do some of that Bobbie, you always sweep."

She handed over the broom. She must have been pleasantly surprised that I was making an effort. It's not that I was a slob, just that all those conventional female duties, like cleaning, didn't have any appeal. It was part of women's oppression, right? Plus these women were more like my grandmother and got the job done before it dawned on me that it needed doing.

That day I swept. Long black strands of women's hair filled the dustpan. They were all over the place. There was so much shedding, it was unbelievable that I hadn't noticed before. We were eight women confined to close quarters, so it was natural for hair to pile up. It was like a horror movie, and I imagined the hair coming to life and strangling me. This was why the ladies in my cell swept so much, and I thought it was merely carrying out the traditional women's role.

What else had I failed to notice? Women cleaning the toilets and showers when the guards brought around the Clorox cleansers once a week. It was surprising that the cleanup tasks were not better shared. No one seemed to resent that some people contributed more than others. Or maybe while I was oblivious in my cell they gossiped about my lack of communal contribution. Taking care of my surroundings as if it was home. It was home for now as much as I rebelled against that idea. I could do better. My breathing deepened and my gerbil whiskers unwound. Out with the red air, in with the blue air.

I went back into my cell to see if my playing cards were there, without feeling like I was hiding out. The cards were safe where I moved them, tucked down in the pillowcase. My letters were scattered all over the bed. They entirely covered the blanket. It was like a thousand one-dollar bills. My wealth. I wondered if the guards were shocked that I had so many letters. I hoped so. I wanted them to know I wasn't the ordinary inmate, even if I didn't want my cellmates to think that. Now I had reason to stay in my cell: to reorganize.

The rest of the day went back to the normal schedule: my version of yoga, picking at supper, calling home, and a visit. When I got back from the visitors area, I added sweeping the dayroom to my routine. It didn't seem like subjugation or replacing home with jail anymore. It connected my multiple realities.

Evening wore on and no one went back to their cells. There was comfort in being close together. And there was something good on TV! The *Houston Post* TV guide said that the movie *The Burning Bed* was on at 8:00 p.m. It starred Farah Fawcett. We all watched it.

The movie was based on a true story of a woman who was repeatedly abused by her spouse for thirteen years. After another night of violence, Farah's movie-husband fell off into deep sleep. Farah got up and put her three children into the car and buckled their seat belts. We watched Farah walk back into the house to the bedroom. She poured gasoline on the bed and lit a match while her husband remained in a stupor. Farah strode back to the car. She drove off with her children to the police station while the house went up in flames. She confessed to killing her husband and was found not-guilty by reason of temporary insanity.

We all cheered and high-fived each other. Go Farah! She was our new hero. The bastard got what he deserved. There was justice after all. Farah restored our dignity. With smiles and hugs we drifted back to our cells as the anguish of the body search melted away.

# Chapter 16
# Is Everything Political?

It was the first week of January. I was sitting in the dayroom with Bobbie, she reading her bible and I *East of Eden*. I'd love to say it was a balmy day, gray or rainy, but unless it was Monday, Wednesday, or Friday, when we went to the roof for recreation, there was no way to know the weather. Weather deprivation, another common overlooked experience that was magnified when missing.

While Bobbie and I shared our weather-less parallel universes, one of the guards came into the cell. Instead of a looking one way and talking the other, she smiled, made eye contact and said, "I have some leftover samples of men's Sure deodorant. They were handed out to the male inmates over the Christmas holidays. Thought the ladies could use them."

I was past having reservation about being on the receiving end of others' charitable deeds. Men's deodorant couldn't be that different than women's deodorant, except for the smell. I pulled off the top and held the deodorant up to my nose. Instead of noticing an odor, I noticed a tiny foam football. It was some kind of advertisement rubber cemented to the side of the deodorant stick. I stroked the football to loosen the glue, and gently peeled it off in one piece. Bobbie had taken a deodorant too, and I asked her, "Mind if I get that foam football thing off your deodorant?"

"Sure. What do you plan to do with it?"

"I'll put them on a letter to my kids. It will be a little post-Christmas treat. They should be coming home from their grandparents' the day after tomorrow."

I retrieved two sheets of blue stationary Josie included when she wrote me last. This was a special occasion. I carefully adhered one foam football to the top of each piece of paper.

When I made out my commissary list before the holidays, I was tempted to buy some extra M&Ms to send to Tony and Pete for a small present. But sending something acquired through the jail system seemed tainted. It was like bringing a virus into the house. The little football novelty was something from the outside world. Even if I got it in jail, it was not infected. It was hardly what anyone would call a gift, but I could imagine my kids smiling when they opened their letters and found a surprise inside.

Thinking how a small present could be significant brought to mind *The White-Haired Girl*. This was one of the first Chinese Communist ballets. When I was in the RCP and saw a film of the performance, I remembered being captivated with the beauty of the dancing and the power of the political message.

In the opening scene of the ballet, Yang, a poor peasant, is desperate to give his daughter, Xi'er, a gift for the Spring Festival. The only thing he can afford is a red ribbon. When Yang gives the ribbon to Xi'er, she throws her hands up and leaps in the air. She vaults from one end of the stage to the other, her eyes never leaving the ribbon as she twirls it overhead. Her exuberant dancing conveys joy and appreciation for the ribbon as if it were a jade necklace.

The athleticism of the dance, the searing expression on the dancers' faces, and the brown, high-collared, Mao-inspired uniform-costumes, confirmed in my mind that only revolutionary art was worthwhile. Art served one class or the other. Art had an underlying political message. If it didn't promote the values and virtues of the workers and peasants, then, by default, it served the capitalists.

Something about lumping all art into propaganda of one sort or another didn't fit anymore. But I didn't understand art without the political template. I was touched by the movement of dancers' bodies floating in space. Visual artists drew me in with vibrant color and intriguing design. The sound of music transformed my surroundings. Written words took me out of myself. Could those experiences have significance of their own? Were there things untouched by class struggle?

The artists at Texas Art Supply who rallied to my case weren't fazed about supporting a former communist who had been all for dictating what was art and what was not—or rather what art would be supported and what would be repressed—not that there was a huge threat of that happening anytime soon.

Becoming political gave me a way to see the impact of class on artist creations. It couldn't be erased. The problem was it became the only way I understood creativity. The grid of proletariat versus capitalist explained it all. At least it did to me at the time.

The emotion that creativity expressed, the power of that emotion to connect us—this was something I was beginning to disconnect from politics, from the politically correct line. The correct line. Line. What was more one-dimensional than that?

I wondered, if I watched *The White-Haired Girl* without my ideological lens, would it still be so appealing? Could I still be moved by the dancers and feel empathy for the peasants or would the propaganda element that once heightened my love for that ballet, glare its superimposed message and be a turn off? I knew some people, a lot, who thought art was not the place for politics. It was about self-expression. It was about the imagination, and politics was like a dead weight that stomped that out. Feelings trumped all. That didn't seem to be enough for my new reality either. Was it possible that all the contradictions of art and politics, in art and politics, were more of a stew? They existed together and influenced each other and everyone has their personal take on how it tastes and what it all means.

If Tony and Pete opened up their letters and their faces lit up upon finding the foam footballs, that's what mattered. It was only a small treat; no more than a surprise in a Cracker Jack box. It was the best I could do, like Yang's red ribbon. The significance was its statement of my love for Tony and Pete. My love for them was pure. Maybe that was all I needed to know.

*January 11, 1986*
*Tom, sweetheart, Tom,*

*The visit this Sunday just tore my heart apart. I held back the tears only because I thought it would be interpreted by the kids as tears of unhappiness, but instead it was tears of longing and love. Seeing you guys hits me like no other thing. I get such a surge of emotion. I so love to see your faces beaming with joy when we visit. I love you guys so utterly. I love you guys without any hesitation or reserve. It is total and encompassing. It's a feeling so strong it touches every nerve in my body. It's like I'm completely riveted to the sight of y'all in the visitation booth and I only pull myself away because I know we'll eventually be reunited. "And what a glorious rebirth that will be."*

*All my love, Betty*

Jail photo used as exhibit in trial

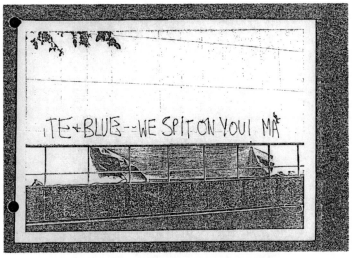

Photo of spray painting used as exhibit in trial

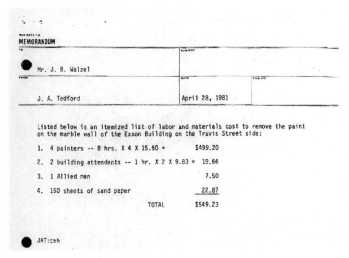

Exxon's list of expenses used as exhibit in trial

# Mother of 2 facing prison for mischief

By KATHERINE KERR
Post Reporter

Betty Sullivan, 36, sits in the Harris County Jail this Thanksgiving awaiting transfer to prison for spray painting an anti-American slogan on a building four years ago.

The mother of two grade-school children faces two years at the Texas Department of Corrections' Gatesville prison for women for a criminal mischief conviction.

Sullivan was convicted in 1981 for spray painting the Exxon Building. She claims she didn't do it.

About 3 a.m. on April 28, 1981, someone spray-painted "Red, White and Blue, we spit on you. Fly the Red Flag First." A cab driver was the only known witness.

Two officers from the Houston Police Department's Criminal Intelligence Division showed the cabbie several pictures of Sullivan, whom they had kept a file on for several years because of her political activities.

**SULLIVAN:** Awaiting prison

The driver identified Sullivan as the person he saw that morning, said Sullivan's attorney, Glen Van Slyke.

Four days later at a May Day rally, Sullivan was among several people arrested. She was told she had been charged with criminal mischief — spray-painting the Exxon building, "which I didn't know anything about," she said.

Van Slyke said Sullivan was at home with her sons that morning. Although she was a political activist for years, Sullivan said she never did anything destructive, much less deface Exxon's building.

Sullivan believed — naively, she says now — that she would never go to jail.

"First of all, I didn't do it and I guess I didn't think I'd get two years' TDC time without probation," she said in a jail interview Wednesday.

Attempts to reach the prosecutor and the judge in the case were not successful.

Although Sullivan said she had little faith in the American judicial system before her trial, she believed she would never see the inside of a prison even if convicted.

Sullivan and her attorney said she didn't get a fair trial because of prejudice against radicals.

Van Slyke said during jury selection state District Judge George Walker would not allow him to tell the jurors what was written on the wall of the Exxon building. He said the jurors were only told that the case had to do with damage to the building and that for all they knew she had rammed her car into the structure.

After the trial began, however, Walker allowed photographs of the slogan on the building to be shown to the jurors over the protest of defense attorneys.

"When we saw their jaws drop we knew she wouldn't get a fair trial," Van Slyke said.

Van Slyke said the charge could have been a misdemeanor. However, the judge allowed Exxon to submit its estimate of the cost to clean up the slogan;

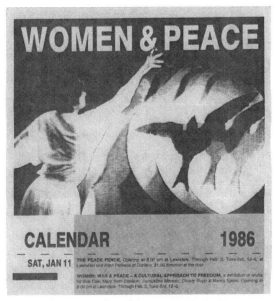

Women and Peace conference flyer
announcing Peace Fence

Drawing of dove made in jail,
displayed on peace fence

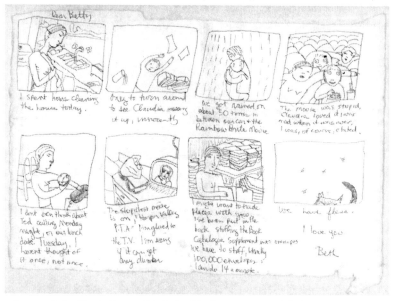

Artwork by Beth Secor, included in letter to me while incarcerated

Cartoon by Texas Art Supply coworkers included in letter to me
while incarcerated

Josie Jenkin's painting of our jail visit

Polaroid taken in prison visiting area
posed next to artificial flowers

My father, Philip Baer, World War II
army photo

My mother, Ruth
Tepper Baer, in her
20s

Betty Sullivan Benefit t-shirt designed by Kevin Bakos

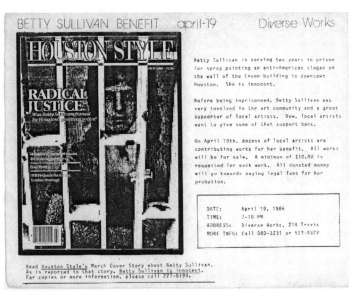

Benefit flyer with picture from *Houston Style* magazine cover

Tony and Peter in Bradford St. house framed with cardboard from
writing pad and yarn

Envelope decorated with love

# Part 3

# Chapter 17
# Away

*January 24, 1986*
*My precious bunch,*

*They have taken you, and I am so afraid for you. I am letting myself hate them some, it is doubly, trebly outrageous. And the fact that you are totally innocent stands out to me now even more sharply than before. Why you? Why are you being made to suffer?*

*I feel that you are so vulnerable now, fragile even. Just a fragile and loving human being. And now totally out of direct touch. My God, love, this is awful. I know you are quite strong, and resilient, capable. I know that, but that doesn't matter right now. What matters is that they have taken you from us and it hurts, it hurts us and it hurts you and it hurts human beings. It is wrong, senseless, unjust and vindictive. You are spending your first night there and you must be terribly down. I wonder what kind of cell they have you in. I wish I could change places with you! Are they singling you out in any way?*

*When I sat tonight, I was almost praying, my heart was chanting secret supplications to protect you. Peter's face was disbelief when I came home from jail tonight. They are both being so good.*

*I talked to Jack, who was quite upset to hear the news. We agreed to contact jail, lawyers, minister, and* *journalist right away. I am putting $20.00 in the mail tomorrow for you and hope it will reach you OK. The kids and I have already planned to come see you the first chance we get.*

*When the kids and I left Gulf Gate for pencils and were home before 5:00 p.m. You hadn't called by 5:15 and my stomach sank, but we still went to Spanky's Pizza for supper. Then I dropped the kids off at basketball. Then I sped to the jail. I went through the very short line and up the elevators and sat down and waited for you to appear. I positioned myself so I could see your approach, your dimension, your reality and objectivity, your flesh-and-blood existence. Even in the blue jail smock you look good, you invest it with such dignity.*

*I sat and anticipated and then a large white woman came out to visit a black man. I saw her in the reflection and realized it wasn't you and my heart sank a little. Then the guard called out my name and asked me to come back to the station, and I knew you were gone.*

*When I came home I started reading the kids a book brother-in-law Kraig sent. Wendy (the reporter) called. Jack had called her, and she was stunned that you had been sent to Gatesville. I asked her to investigate and find out where you are and let them know that she knows you are in there, and she was glad to help.*

*I'll call broadly tomorrow. We are with you, your pain is our pain, and your joy will be our joy.*

*All our love, TB and the boys*

## January 22, 1986. Wednesday night.

As I lay curled up on my bunk bed, I didn't hear the main cell doors clank open. The sound of footsteps entering my personal cell seemed like part of a dream. No one comes into my cell. My eyelids were pulled shut, yet I couldn't ignore the weight of a hand on my shoulder rocking me.

"Get ready, Betty, you're moving to Gatesville. If you want to keep your letters, I'll give you a box that you can address and we'll send them to your home. You don't need to bring anything with you."

The guard set down a small cardboard box, a black marker, and packing tape on the floor next to my bed.

"I'll be back for you in ten minutes," she said, walking out of my cell.

This must be pullin' chain. The fuzziness in my mind cleared as I sat up and stretched. I had ten minutes and, in the luxury of that time, thought about my friends as I carefully packed their letters. So many of them had shared what was bubbling under the surface. Writing me gave them a chance to express what was hard to verbalize. Marion wrote about the hurt she felt when her in-laws were always praising her husband's first wife, and how he didn't get that at all when she told him how she felt. Jim confided in me that he worried about his attraction to other men. Susan was suspicious of her husband's late-night phone calls and wondered where her marriage was headed.

I remembered hearing about the Sabbath candlesticks, the only possession of value my grandmother brought with her from the "Old Country" when she immigrated to the United States with the great wave of Eastern Europeans in the early 1900s. My letters were the material connection to my world. As much as I feared parting with those letters, I had confidence that new ones would follow me wherever I went. It was the only thing I was confident about.

I printed my home address on top of the box. According to procedure the postage would be charged to my commissary account. I must have enough money in there. I hoped they wouldn't get lost. When I worked at the Post Office, I was shocked that the majority of mail made it to the right destination. It did, though, it did.

The only defense against being uprooted like a refugee was positive self-talk. Each day was one day behind me. "I Will Survive" became my mantra. As terrible as jail was, my confused, neurotic, alienated, self had made it this far. In with the good air, out with the bad air.

I looked over towards Bobbie's cell and silently said goodbye. I envied her belief in God and how that underlying principle made sense of the chaos in the world. Marxism was as close to a bible as I ever had, even if I called it science, not faith. Science implied knowing; belief implied, well, faith. The view that the material world, the natural world, that we as humans are part of is understandable without any recourse to the supernatural was not a belief system, as I had understood it, but simply the truth. Understanding the world without a specific God-presence still made sense to me, but the truth didn't seem so simple anymore. Belief systems and science didn't sound contradictory. The old me would have seen Bobbie's belief in God as a failing, not something to envy. Was my own experience of despair making any belief acceptable? Were knowing and believing that much different? Or was I more tolerant of others' views, of the mystery? I wanted to believe there were things that were true. But I didn't want to push away doubt.

When the guard came back and snapped handcuffs on my wrists it was a relief to get out of the puzzle in my head and move on: Commence pullin' chain.

I looked the guard in the eye when she turned to face me. "My letters are all packed. Please make sure they get sent home."

"I understand. They'll get home, and you will too. Ready to go?"

"Yes, thanks." Reassurance from the guards was not typical, and I welcomed those words.

I was escorted through the jail maze. The gerbil emerged again. We passed through endless corridors and steel-barred doors. Video cameras and lights were set high in the crumbling ceiling. Keys rattled with each door being unlocked and locked until we reached an elevator. Down we went to a small, stuffy room where I met up with four other inmates. Whiskers twitching I checked them out, my hidden superpower to sniff out a situation. I wasn't any gerbil, I was Super Gerbil. Not that there was anything to sniff out. The women looked weary-eyed, each woken up in the middle of the night from cellblocks scattered throughout the jail. The county jail. A chamber of horrors. Good riddance.

"Where ya'll going?" I asked. Silence. "Just a joke."

We were led through a small tunnel into an underground garage where a school bus repurposed as prison transportation was waiting. We lined up, practically on top of each other, as the guards hovered like sheepdogs making sure no one from the herd made a run for it. I stepped up and onto the bus, guided by a guard with a paw on my back. As the last of the group boarded, the driver slammed the door shut and turned on the ignition.

The garage door creaked opened and the bus emerged onto the quiet downtown street. I couldn't remember the last time I'd seen empty city streets. Was it on a still night like this that the Exxon building got spray-painted? It would be fitting if we passed by it on the way to I-10. Of course we didn't.

The bus followed the ramp to the deserted freeway and headed west until we merged onto highway 290. The sky grew darker as we distanced ourselves from the glare of the city lights.

Even if there wasn't much to see except shadows and grey-black sky, I wouldn't allow myself to doze off, and forced my blinking eyes open. The color reminded me of the Mark Rothko paintings in the Rothko Chapel next to the Menil Museum. Black with shades of deep violet and steel-grey, at first look it was more a void than a color. But after starring at the paintings, dots of darkness and light swirled in and out of the canvas. Following the movement of color, it was never clear whether what I was seeing was really there or a trick that Mark Rothko played.

Even as a communist, visiting the Rothko Chapel exerted an unexpected force on me. I was not attracted to quiet and contemplation, but I found myself going to visit the Rothko Chapel repeatedly. One day I took my kids there and explained that the enormous, dark, abstract paintings were the last thing that Mark Rothko did before he committed suicide. Pete responded, "If I painted like that, I'd kill myself too."

I used to think Pete's response was hysterical. Now I wondered what kind of mother I was, talking about suicide to my young child.

With that disturbing thought I fell into a fitful sleep. My escape hatch took me back down to my own past.

* * *

It all started after I graduated from The Wheatley School, on Long Island, a public high school with a private-sounding name. Senior year, my best friend Lynn was beginning to question the prevailing suburban bourgeois norms we were born into. Not me. I lusted after a megaphone charm and won the last place on my high school cheerleading squad.

That all changed in September 1967. I started college at New York University (NYU) University Heights. This was part of, but not the same as, the very cool NYU in Greenwich Village.

NYU uptown, as we called it, was an oasis in the Bronx, a lush green campus of fifty acres overlooking the Harlem River. The domed library, the centerpiece of the Classical-style architecture buildings, was framed by a circular arch called the Hall of Fame for Great Americans. This was an open colonnade dotted with bronze busts that included, along with George Washington and Eli Whitney, Booker T. Washington, Susan B. Anthony, and Henry David Thoreau. This was a temple of learning, though not an elite institution.

I had a B- average in high school. My mother never went beyond high school and my father received an accounting degree from a two-year program at City College of New York.

At NYU there were three small all-girls dorms on campus, and I lived in one of them. On the first day at school, I unpacked my suitcase and arranged my stuffed animals on my twin bed. I was cautiously anticipating college. I had no clue about a major. Math and science were my favorite subjects, not that it meant anything. My brother John was the science genius of the family, a bit of a mad scientist with a tangle of beakers and test tubes spewing from his monster chemistry set. I was never jealous. He was always good to me, and comparing my intellect to John's never crossed my mind. He was a boy and supposed to be smart. My plan, the prevailing wisdom for girls of my generation, was to get an M.R.S. and catch a nice Jewish doctor.

Without much on my mind, I set out from my dorm, walking across the quadrangle for orientation in the Hall of Languages. I followed the other freshmen filing into the lecture auditorium for our first introduction to college life, and took a seat. That funny feeling where you think someone is staring at you came over me. I swiveled my head around and noticed a skinny guy with curly, light brown hair sitting two rows down, looking in my direction. Even with other students between us, I prickled at a wave of heat coming my way.

The next day, as I stood in the checkout line at the bookstore, this mystery boy approached me in his faded denim jacket and bell-bottom jeans. My hair was in a flip and I was wearing pedal pushers and a seersucker blouse.

"What are you buying?" he asked, sounding like he already knew me.

"Just freshman English, math," I said. "You know, the usual stuff."

"Hey, I see an Intro to Philosophy book in there, too."

"Oh, yeah, well, I'm taking that class. I don't know what I want to major in and so maybe this will help me figure it out."

"You sound pretty smart."

I hadn't thought of myself as smart. That compliment was pure flattery.

He told me his name was Lee, and followed me out of the bookstore, becoming more animated with his impish freckles jumping around his face.

"Have you heard about the anti-Vietnam War protest on campus tomorrow?" he asked.

I hadn't considered politics as having much to do with my world, but Vietnam was getting a lot of news coverage. I was curious to know what it all meant, and Lee was cute.

"No. Are you going?" I asked.

"Yeah, you should come with me."

That was our first date.

The next day at 4:00 p.m. we met up with a small group of students in the quadrangle getting ready for the on-campus march. The chess club and student government had tables set up as part of orientation. The campus radicals planned a protest before the first day of classes. They were as eager to expose the new freshman to the budding anti-war movement as the more conventional clubs were to recruit members.

Poster board signs saying, "Stop the War Now!" were passed out. Lee and I each took a sign and hoisted it up in the air. At the head of the group stood a super-skinny guy with a scraggly beard. Lee pointed to him and said, "That's Dennis. I met him the other day. He's starting a chapter of SDS on campus." Without a clue what SDS was, I nodded like I knew exactly what he was talking about.

Dennis raised a bullhorn to his lips and said, "Let's get started!" Lee glanced at me with his reassuring smile, took my free hand, and off we went.

We marched around campus, shouting, "Hell No We Won't Go!" and "One, Two, Three, Four, We Won't Fight Your Fucking War!" Some of the onlookers gave us the peace sign. We shot them the peace sign back, saying, "Right on!" A few in the march held up their clenched fists.

In the beginning I felt like I was tagging along. Then I found my voice and chimed in, chanting softly, then as forcefully as I could. It came easily with Lee's approving nods to cheer me on.

After that first march, there were meetings and protests every weekend. My initial self-consciousness was overtaken by a feeling that I was part of something important and bigger than me. I was taking a stand. I didn't know much about Vietnam, but I was open-minded. I felt like a sponge, absorbing new and exciting information about the world around me and doing something about it, too! My heart quickened. I didn't know whether this was from being with Lee or participating in a budding mass movement. The passions were intertwined.

Lee was light on his feet and his body so compact he seemed to prance, not walk. I could spot him on the far side of the campus quadrangle, elfin and in motion. He spent hours planning demonstrations and I helped making signs and banners. He stayed up reading all night and seemed to know everything about world politics. He was sexy and sophisticated and made me feel desirable in a way that was totally new. To top it off Lee was Jewish, half of that Jewish doctor my parents longed for me to become the M.R.S. of.

Lee lived on the fourth floor of a five-story walk-up in a small apartment off campus. Posters of Huey Newton and Bob Dylan livened up the walls. Peeling paint was taken over by the March on Washington, the Grateful Dead, Malcolm X, Country Joe and the Fish, and a Mets pennant. Leaving the tidy girls' dorm on campus and walking up to Lee's place was crossing into a Bohemian underground.

Lee loved to explain things, which made me feel less stupid asking questions. He the teacher; me the student. I racked my brain, trying to understand why he cast his love-light on me. All I knew was that I was the luckiest girl on earth when Lee's kiss turned my world from black and white to psychedelic.

Lee and I and the other NYU radicals all joined SDS (Students for a Democratic Society). By that time I was picking up the language and ideas of the New American Left. SDS had a broad agenda: against the Vietnam War, nuclear war, the arms race, and discrimination. They promoted nonviolent civil disobedience. SDS did not exclude communists, but it was nowhere near a communist-front organization, as some would have you believe.

One NYU campus protest was particularly memorable. To expose the horrors of Agent Orange, used as a defoliant in Vietnam, we passed out flyers saying that a dog would be subjected to this harsh chemical to see how it would be affected. The day of the protest brought out many people who wouldn't ordinarily show up, but were beside themselves that anyone would do such a thing to an innocent dog. In the middle of the quadrangle was a small brown mutt, pink tongue panting and tail wagging. Dennis held him on a leash with one hand, a bullhorn in the other hand. More and more students gathered to see what was going on.

"If those radicals do something to that dog, they've lost all my support."

"I can't believe they would be so heartless. Just when I thought there was some truth to what they were saying about Vietnam."

I was a little worried myself. I was growing confident that my involvement in the movement went beyond Lee, but the rally made me nervous. Seeing Dennis with the dog, I was torn. Would he really hurt a dog to make a point about the death and destruction in Vietnam? Would this be a test of my loyalties to the cause? Dennis, the leader of our SDS chapter, had planned this piece of the protest alone. The rest of our group was in as much suspense as everyone else.

More and more people milled around. We radicals were handing out flyers proclaiming that Vietnam was as a just war of liberation, but everyone had their eyes on the dog. Dennis seemed to be stalling. Minutes passed. Was he not sure what to do?

At last Dennis lifted his bullhorn and spoke to the crowd:

"We have no intention of harming this sweet dog, so relax. But check out your own reaction. If you are outraged that a dog would be subject to Agent Orange, what about all the civilians in Vietnam getting sprayed with the poison?"

I was so relieved when Dennis said those words. Dennis would rage about the war, but of course he wouldn't hurt a dog.

As a member of SDS, I took myself and my mission seriously. I evolved from being a student of Lee's to a student of the revolution. I studied *Labor's Untold Story* by Richard Boyer and Herbert Morais; *The People's History of the United States* by Howard Zinn; *The Autobiography of Malcolm X* by Alex Haley and Malcolm X; *The Wretched of the Earth* by Frantz Fanon. I learned there was an "old left" revolving around the Communist Party U.S.A. (CPUSA). These people, Americans who called themselves communists and cheered the Russian revolution, also helped build labor unions and actively supported the civil rights movement. The CPUSA exposed and fought against the racist frame-up of the Scottsboro Boys in Alabama.

I learned the "new left" thought that Russia had fallen off the socialist to communist path and favored Mao Zedong and the Chinese Revolution. William Hinton, an American farmer and Marxist, traveled to China and wrote *Fanshen*, praising Mao's land reform policies. *Away with All Pests*, by American surgeon Joshua Horn, praised collective healthcare after his visit to China. Mao was the leader of the Long March that liberated millions from feudal oppression in China. These were the stories, events, and heroes that shaped my thinking. Instead of associating the word "communist" with bad people doing despicable deeds, I took communist to mean good people fighting for a better life for all.

All the study and activism built up my confidence and ego. Even if I wasn't personally oppressed, I felt connected to the long tradition of leftist intellectuals, many of them communists, many of them Jews. Their legacy of fighting for justice and a just society was my inheritance. The empowering idea that society could be radically changed to serve the people had taken hold.

My parents drove to the Bronx to pick me up the first time I came home on college break. I was a changed person. The crisp, new clothes for college that I had left home in were replaced with dirty bell-bottom jeans and a tie-dyed t-shirt. My red hair was liberated from being ironed and rolled on soup cans to being frizzy and free.

After the quiet ride home, my father parked the Oldsmobile in the garage. I ran into the house and called Lynn. She went to Bard College. I was eager to show off how far I progressed from being a know-nothing cheerleader. She and a group of high school friends were meeting that night at the house of someone whose parents would be trustingly out for the evening.

After my parents took me out for supper, Lynn came by and picked me up in her parents' Datsun. In those four months since we graduated, the playing field had leveled. Everyone was a hippie. That night I smoked my first joint to the tune of Jimi Hendrix's "Are You Experienced," and fit right in. As my political activism grew, my drug use went from a minor part of my life to non-existent. Being involved in radical politics meant drugs were off limits. Getting busted for pot was not worth the risk.

The next evening I stayed home with my parents as promised. My mother prepared my favorite meal of rare roast beef. My brother was not there. After he graduated from Tufts, he went into the Peace Corps, in Tanzania, which I admired him for. He would bring back my first Mao buttons as China provided foreign aid and technical assistance in building the Tanzania-

Zambia Railway as a way to support decolonized African countries. This paved the way for China to develop trade in an underdeveloped part of the world. I was sure it was purely altruistic. Those authentic Mao buttons were the envy of all my radical friends.

I constructed my roast beef into a sandwich with fresh rye bread. My mother ordinarily expressed outrage that I was demeaning the choice cut of meat by turning it into a sandwich. This time she made no comment.

My mom said, "Tell us all about your classes."

"Um, I'm taking English, Algebra 2, Intro to World History, and Intro to Philosophy."

"Sounds like you're learning something," my dad said.

"You know, Dad, I'm learning a lot, but it's more about how wrong the war in Vietnam is than what I get from my classes."

"I'm not so sure about the war, either," he said.

"That's great! I'm so glad you don't believe all the propaganda."

I went on to lecture them about how rotten our government was. How people of color all over the world were taking back their countries from colonial powers. How the wealth we had in this country was built off the oppression of people in other countries. How our so-called democracy at home only masked the true aims of profits-at-any-cost. They couldn't get a word in edgewise, even if they tried.

"Have you heard that families in the U.S. are adopting Vietnamese war orphans to make up for the crimes of U.S. imperialism? Doesn't that sound like a good idea for you?"

That got a response out of them.

"But your Dad and I are really too old to start to raise a child now," my mother said.

"That's a cop out, Mom. It's the least you can do to take responsibility for war in Vietnam."

My Mom and Dad exchanged worried glances. They had no idea what had come over me. I'm sure they were aware of the transformation that youth of that era were going through. It must have seemed akin to the body snatchers. Where did our Betty go? On the other hand, my parents were liberal Democrats, hardly war hawks or restrictive. Little did they know that this was only the beginning.

* * *

The bus rumbled along. I rubbed my eyes open and saw that the midnight-blue sky had dissipated and the sun started to rise. The blood orange dawn lifted the dark sky. It pulled me up. I sat with my spine erect and planted my nose against the cool bus window. My sensory-deprived eyes took in the rolling, golden hills, backlit by morning sun. The central Texas prairie went on for miles and miles. Far in the distance white geometric shapes reflected back the sun. My body crumpled down in to the seat cushion as I registered what was before me.

The prison bus rounded one last hill as the outline of Gatesville took shape. Tall, white guard towers rose from an expanse of sage-green fields. Beyond the concertina wire fence, the broad lawn was dotted with one-story, white buildings. It could be mistaken for a college campus, except there were no students bustling through the grounds. The eerie quiet seeped through the bus—until we made our final approach. Barking greyhounds appeared out of nowhere and prison guards surrounded the bus as we went through the main gate at the central guard tower. Another gate slammed down behind us. In our locked-down position, paperwork was exchanged by the bus driver and the prison guards. We were counted and recounted. Livestock corralled into the stockyards.

At last we were led out of the bus and lined up at the start of a long corridor linking the bus drop off point to the entryway for Gatesville prison. As we approached our destination, the diagnostic unit, a voice screeched, "Get your fucking hands off me." The line skidded to a stop. We rear-ended each other, then bolted upright to rubberneck the commotion. At the far end of the hallway, several guards were dragging a woman towards us. She was in handcuffs and leg irons, screaming, "Let me go, you assholes." Her elbows and hair swung in opposite directions. One of the guards held a video camera recording the action. In an instant she was hustled out some secret door. It happened so quickly and was so intense that I wondered if I imagined the whole thing. I swiveled to see the other women in line. Their faces were lit up like mine. No, this was real. If this was what prison was really like, I was never going to survive. My hands instantly sweaty, I sucked in a deep breath through my nose and contributed to a collective gulp.

"Come along, ladies." The guard's words broke the spell. I stared ahead and shuffled along with the chainless chain gang to my new residence.

At the end of the passageway was a rectangular room lined with long, wooden benches. We were told to take a seat and wait to get searched, our mug shot taken, and fingerprinted, before we were christened with the new term "offender" and became property of TDC.

Looking around I noticed the ladies in the room were predominantly white. Gatesville was the sole women's prison in Texas. Women were funneled from local county jails all across the state, encompassing a huge rural area. As the minutes turned to hours, and weight-shifting was not helping the numb feeling traveling from my butt to my brain, a new group of women arrived. The one that sat down beside me said: "Where did you fall from?"

I gave her a puzzled look.

"Fell from, girl, that's what we call it here, where did you come from?"

"I'm from Houston."

"You're lucky you come from a big city. I fell from the Jasper County Jail. East Texas. See my two black eyes? I got beat up by those MF jailers. Got a broken nose and broken ribs too. I was the only woman in that small shithole and those rednecks took it out on me. Fuck, I thought they'd have sympathy for their own kind. You'd think it was a crime to be a woman the way they treated me."

"That's awful. Can you do anything about that?"

"You are kidding me, aren't you? I'd only get in more trouble."

"It's still not right."

"Hell, I know that."

A monstrous punch hit me. I had never encountered any woman beaten up by a man, jailer or not.

She looked me up and down and said: "You ever get in a fight?"

"Can't say I've been in a fight."

"You married?"

"Yes."

"Got any kids?"

"I have two sons."

"They gotta fight."

"Not really, they argue, but don't hit each other. I can't imagine my husband ever trying to hurt me."

"That's new to me. No fighting? Even with boys? It's the way of the world. Are you putting me on?"

"No, really, it's true. Oh, but I once threw a punch at someone from the Socialist Worker's party at a rally many years ago. I had just started taking karate lessons and it made me feel tough. Are you married?"

"The Socialist what? Hell yeah, I'm married. My old man gets drunk and, truth is, with the both of us drinking, I can't keep track of who starts it, but there's some swinging going on. Doesn't mean we don't love each other. That's the reason I'm in here now. Car theft. He'd be locked up for a long time if I didn't take the rap.

"Taking the rap for your husband. Now that's real sacrifice."

"Women always sacrifice for their man. It's the way of the world.

# Chapter 18
# Who is a Feminist?

While incarcerated in the Harris County Jail, I wiped my butt and took a shower in full view of the other inmates and guards. I never got used to it, but I did it, like everything else we think we can't do until there is no choice. When I was transferred to the women's prison in Gatesville, privacy was paramount. Not only did we have doors on the toilet stalls and shower curtains, we were not allowed to be seen without our clothes on. This total turnaround had nothing to do with bestowing dignity on the offenders; the real cause was that in the 1980s, homosexuality was illegal in the prison system.

The diagnostic unit is the first stop for new arrivals when they enter the "Big House." Our initial activity was watching orientation videos describing the rules in prison. One of the videos explained what happened if you got caught engaging in homosexual activity. The first time, you received a reprimand. The second time was another reprimand. If there was a third reprimand, you got saddled with a case. A case meant that charges could be filed against you. Reprimand, case, charges, it all sounded serious, frightening, too. Worse, what explicitly was considered homosexual activity was never spelled out. And you can bet no one asked.

Having a tad of humanity thrown back at me, whatever the reason, was a thawing of sorts. I had coped with the lack of privacy by turning myself into an automaton. Not having to shut down my embarrassment at nakedness was a relief, but it came with some logistical costs. We had to get dressed behind closed doors.

The diagnostic unit was composed of a large, open room lined with twenty high and skinny bunk beds. At one end was the smaller communal area with the TV. The showers and toilets were behind doors in another area off the dorm, like you'd see in a gym.

Our prison-issued tote bags hung on the back of the short metal frame post at the head of the bunk beds. They held our temporary wardrobe (we would get a permanent uniform later), prison issued toilet paper and toiletries. Toilet paper was considered part of our personal property and we had to bring it with us when using the commode.

Morning ritual started at 4:00 a.m. A gray uniformed guard appeared at the door. "Time to get up and get ready for breakfast." Collective eye-rubbing, yawning, and stretching followed. In unison we grabbed what we needed from our tote bags. Since I had a top bunk, I had the extra challenge of propelling my body down a shaky ladder with my bundle of supplies. After my feet safely touched the floor, I headed into the bathroom/shower area. I waited in line to dress behind either the toilet stall doors or shower curtains, safely out of public view.

After getting dressed, we went back to the dorm to deposit our sleepwear and toilet supplies—up the ladder to the bunk bed and down again. I followed the migration, and went out a door and down a paved walkway towards a separate building that served as a mess hall.

Without quite knowing how it happened, I was outside. Stars dotted the dark sky. It was amazing!

We proceeded down the walk, lined up in pairs or "deuced," per prison slang. Two guards escorted us, one in front and one in back of our procession. I was thrilled to find out we went outdoors three times a day to and from meals.

Despite the feeling of being on a POW death march, the crisp morning breeze lifted my spirits. I gazed up and shivered, imagining my kids and Tom seeing the same starry sky. We shared this space outside of ourselves. This earth. This air. This sky. Instead of the sinking feeling that dragged me down in jail, this felt like floating. I walked along with my head back, hoping not to trip or bump into anyone. I couldn't let go of the sensation that if I just kept looking up, I would be transported to another dimension.

The agriculture schedule duplicated in the county jail made a little more sense here. The prison operated as self-sufficiently as possible. Offenders worked in the fields surrounding the dorms. They harvested mustard and collard greens, cabbage and bush beans. They fattened pigs and groomed horses. Some even rode horses. This was rural Texas, after all. The prison and the country setting, minus the concertina wire and guard towers, were farm-like.

The deuced line followed through the open cafeteria door to a room filled with long, white tables and matching folding chairs. I picked up my tray and flatware and joined the service line, the pungent smell of grease replacing the intoxicating air.

Breakfast typically consisted of eggs, biscuits, coffee, and sausages. Other than a heavy hand in the lard department, it was better than anything at the county jail. Offenders prepared and served the food, their pride reflected in cooking up something with substance and flavor. The women serving on the other side of the line dished out generous helpings of jiggling eggs and glistening sausage with wide smiles. I tried to twist my frown back into a smile. Was I the only one worried about stuffing my face with copious calories? I didn't want to be picky. I remembered in the orientation video that we were expected to finish whatever we had on our tray. Breakfast was my favorite meal, but I couldn't imagine eating like this every day.

We were allowed only twenty minutes to gobble down all of our food. As I scoffed down my biscuits and sucked down my black coffee, I turned in the direction of a woman with honey-colored hair falling from her shoulders, hovering over me.

"Can I sit next to you?" she asked.

"OK."

"You're pretty new here, right?"

"Yeah, I fell from Houston yesterday," I proudly said. "How about you?"

"I've been here close to a week. Came from Amarillo."

Her name was Sandra.

We finished our meals and followed back, deuced, to the dorm without another word.

At lunch, which was 10:30 a.m. like the county jail and called supper, Sandra sat by me again.

This time her eyes bored through mine.

"Has anyone told you who to stay away from?"

"No, everyone seems pretty OK, so far."

"There's more going on than you might realize."

Sandra began eating her breakfast, and I wasn't sure if I should be suspicious of her or appreciate that she seemed to be concerned about me. I was afraid to ask her what I should be afraid of, but I didn't want to end the conversation. I desperately needed someone to talk to.

I had learned in the county jail that family was something all of us had in common and that sharing our misery at being banished from home could forge a common bond.

"Gatesville seems better than the jail I came from, but it's so far from where I live. I miss my husband and kids so much," I said. "They used to visit me all the time, but now I heard we only get visits on the weekends. What about you, have any family?"

"I've got people, but no husband or kids." Sandra resumed eating and that was the end of our supper conversation. Maybe bringing up family wasn't the best idea. I didn't see her until breakfast the next day and was relieved when she chose to sit down beside me again.

"Do you see those bull dykes over there looking at me?" Sandra said.

My nose twitched. "Bull dyke" was so politically incorrect.

Sandra continued, "They keep checking me out."

I turned to see whom she was talking about, but only observed a sea of women, heads down, forking food into their mouths. No one seemed to be checking out Sandra. I heard in the county jail to watch out for women with beards in Gatesville. No one had a beard that I saw. Sandra didn't seem like the paranoid type, so I took her word for it and shook my head up and down in agreement.

"I told Gina I wouldn't mess around as long as she didn't either. She's supposed to drive here every weekend to visit. I'll see what happens with that promise. But in the meantime I want to lay low."

After a long pause I asked, "So, how long have you and Gina been, um, together?"

"On and off for a while. I've spent time in the county jail, but not here. This place isn't so bad except for being surrounded by ignorant Blacks and Mexicans. Amarillo isn't like that."

I coughed, trying not to choke on my food. I was embarrassed that Sandra was mouthing off racist comments. Disappointed too.

When Sandra first mentioned Gina, it gave me hope. Meeting up with a lesbian, I thought she would be a kindred spirit. I presumed, from my experience on the left, that lesbians were all radical feminists. But Sandra sounded like a redneck. Sisterhood was about inclusion. Didn't she know that? I was confused, but curious, too, in a Margaret Mead kind of way.

Sandra continued, "If we hang together, those bull dykes will keep off of me."

I was relieved there wasn't more racial commentary, but the term bull dyke still offended me. Maybe that was insider talk. Either way I'd give her a pass as she was from the Texas panhandle and my new philosophy was not to judge, even if it made me appear politically incorrect. At least she wasn't asking me to join some Aryan club.

"Sure, we can hang out together," I said more eagerly than I realized, considering I wasn't even sure what I was agreeing to. What if hanging out with a lesbian would be considered homosexual activity? That fear left quickly. Having someone to connect to trumped any vague notion of reprimands, cases or charges.

I couldn't figure Sandra out. She had a self-confidence about her. She didn't make conversation to fill up space. She was the last to look away when making eye contact. She didn't censor what came out of her mouth— although maybe she should have.

Her tissue-paper-pink skin didn't show a wrinkle, freckle, or the wear of living. It didn't seem possible that she had had an easy life, even if she didn't spend her teenage years sprawled out in the backyard lathed in baby oil working on her tan, like I did. Her skin seemed too good for her age, which she never revealed.

Hanging out with Sandra, I wondered if it was supposed to make us look like a couple or her straight. Most of the hanging out was with your own kind. If I hung with Sandra, would lesbians think I was a lesbian? Or would the straight women think she was straight? Not that I could tell the difference.

Even without talking about it, Sandra correctly assumed I was not tuned in to the sexuality vibe in prison. I felt like a nerdy guy a head cheerleader picks up to get back at her football star boyfriend, without a clue what role I was playing. Being around Sandra made me feel like I was in a mysterious drama. I was happy to be singled out for whatever ride I was along for. It was better than no ride at all.

Sandra and I regularly met up at meals, sat and ate together without talking. I was less inclined to ask her about herself, since I didn't know how to react to her potentially inappropriate comments. Sandra seemed satisfied to be seen with me and nothing more.

One day over breakfast, Sandra informed me she got her assignment to a general population unit and would be leaving soon. This wasn't any surprise as we all knew our stay in the diagnostic was temporary. Still it jolted me. I felt attached to Sandra, even though it was role-play for her and sociology for me. Margaret Mead was replacing gerbil girl. As our time was short, I finally got up the nerve to ask her what had been bugging me.

"What do you think about feminism?" I asked in a pass-the-salt manner.

Sandra hesitated for the first time since we met, then said, "I don't think anything about feminism. I don't hate men, I just like women."

"I think you've got it wrong, feminism isn't about hating men," I said.

"So what is it?"

"For one it's about women's rights and respect and..."

"I have the same rights as anybody else," she bristled. "Nobody's going to mess with me."

"I know that. But what about women in general? Don't you think women are treated like second-class citizens?"

"Never thought about it. If they are, then it's just because they don't have any guts, and I can't help that."

"But doesn't it make you mad when women are taken advantage of?"

She shrugged. "People get taken advantage of all the time. It only pisses me off when it happens to me. And I know how to take care of myself."

This didn't make sense. Sandra was willful and stood up for herself, great, but she didn't have much sympathy for other women. Yet she loved a woman.

"So if you hear about a woman getting beat up by a man, you're fine with that?"

"Give me a break, that's entirely different. I know all about abuse from men. They can all go to hell as far as I'm concerned. But I get mad at the women who sit and take it, too."

It sounded like she was blaming the victim. How dare she find fault with women when they were the object of oppression? This was beyond not being a feminist. Or was she goading me? It wasn't as if she was defending men. She was frustrated that women were passive. She expected more. That could be her way of seeing women as having the potential to be strong, not helpless. But it didn't sound very supportive. I couldn't accept that Sandra wasn't a feminist like she was supposed to be.

When I was a communist, I was convinced that women's equality would be achieved when the whole working class was liberated. When Mao Zedong came to power, he prohibited the centuries-old practice of binding women's feet. Mao's wife was a powerful leader in the Cultural Revolution and a member of the notorious Gang of Four. One of the revolution's slogans was "Women hold up half the sky."

Communists, though, were not known for their support of gay rights. I was embarrassed that when I was in the RCP it didn't seem like a big deal.

Sandra didn't make some political decision to be a lesbian. She didn't consider herself part of the women's liberation movement. She knew who she was. She knew whom she loved. She spoke her mind. If "the personal is political," then she was as feminist as any idea of feminism.

My personal life had been dominated by radical politics, but my relationships were fairly conventional. That I was swept off my feet and into the movement by

Lee, my first love, haunted me. If it was the same old story, women following men, what did that say about my ability to think for myself? In the SDS chapter I belonged to at NYU, most of the women were making the signs and banners for the next protest, while the men were devising strategies and making speeches. I revered the national women leaders of SDS, like Bernadette Dohrn, but I didn't aspire to any position of leadership myself. I didn't equate being behind the scenes with not being liberated, but with choice. Yet was my choice to be behind the scenes a reflection of being unliberated?

After Lee and I broke up, I hooked up with Joe, who was his roommate. I wondered if, looked at in a certain way, I was a piece of furniture that stayed with the apartment. When Joe and I were first married, we shared housework and cooking until Tony and Pete were born. We both were thrilled to be parents and considered Tony and Pete a mutual joy. Yet the domestic duties shifted increasingly into my domain. I didn't mind the more traditional division of labor. Being a mom gave me unexpected purpose. Joe was a good cook, but as the theoretician in the family, his time was more valuable.

As for Tom, I had more clout in that relationship. I was the strong single mother figure, taking on the world. Then I went to prison and saw myself as powerless and needy. Tom was on the outside, protecting and holding the family together. My friends questioned whether me being in prison was about protecting him, but I thought they were all wrong.

Other than visitors, there were no men to be seen in Gatesville. All of the staff was female and the men's prisons were nowhere near Gatesville. There were no chance encounters like the trip to rooftop recreation in the county jail. For those offenders stuck in prison for any length of time, it seemed natural to yearn for an intimate bond. My Margaret Meade persona wondered how many women in prison formed attachments to other women that they would not have in their ordinary lives. Prison may have provided an opportunity to tap into some long-suppressed desire or add spice and adventure to an otherwise numbing existence: a crush, not wanting to get caught and the excitement of walking that thin line. There was plenty of room for imagination behind bars.

Despite the reprimands, cases, and charges to discourage homosexuality, when offenders were allowed to use the commissary, many bought bandanas. It was common knowledge that if you knotted your bandana in a certain way, it would indicate you were "available." Some women clearly eyed each other and brushed shoulders to indicate interest. What other activities went on was too covert for me to decipher. The guards didn't seem very concerned during their daily herding.

At Sandra's last meal in diagnostic she asked me for a hug. We both got up and held on to an embrace. Several women looked our way. If Sandra was putting on a final show, I choose to think that she was genuinely sad to part with me. If the other women were jealous, good. As unperceptive as I perceived myself, Sandra's solid squeeze signaled to me that there was an exchange of caring and respect. I remember telling her about being arrested for spray painting, and she responded, "You go girl!" rather than, "Huh?" She said that spray painting was common practice with the rebels she grew up with.

"I'll write you when I get to my new dorm and tell you if I see any women with goatees," she laughed.

It might sound strange, but women regularly wrote to other women in different parts of the prison, kind of like extended family. Some became pen pals for years. I wondered if Sandra would actually write to me. It would prove that we had had more than a faux friendship, but even if she didn't, I knew Sandra had left a lasting impression that nothing could erase.

# Chapter 19
# Population

During the days in diagnostic, I proceeded down an assembly line, receiving a physical, shots, psychological tests, and interviews. I silently cried out, "Stop, I'm not going to be here that long," yet the conveyor belt rolled on as I was poked, prodded, and probed.

After I went through the rounds of testing, the powers that be would analyze the data and the severity of my crime, and determine what area of general population I would ultimately reside in. The prison population was divided into maximum, medium, and minimum security units. Could the State of Texas be out to get me and put me in a maximum security unit? I had been naive about going to jail in the first place, so nothing short of the electric chair seemed off limits.

My last task before being classified and moving from the diagnostic unit to "population," as we called it, was being measured for "whites": white, elastic-strapped pants and white, v-neck, pullover tops, the prison equivalent to scrubs. This uniform was our permanent offender garb.

I received three pairs of whites. The drill was, one to wear, one to keep in the lock box, and one to send to the laundry. Everybody ironed their whites. It wasn't a rule, just what you did. First razors and then heavy hot irons; you'd think in a prison environment these would be considered potential weapons.

I hated ironing. I never ironed my whites without grumbling and searing the tips of my fingers, making crooked creases. I could accept that in a community of women, it helped the general morale if we all kept ourselves up. I could accept that how you looked and what you wore were time-honored ways for women to define themselves. And the women in prison needed all the help in the self-confidence department that they could get. I've even heard that for some women, ironing is a relaxing ritual.

Here I was different again. If I had my way, we'd all wear wrinkled whites, keep our hair untamed, and dump the makeup. This was prison. Who the hell cares what we look like? For me it was freedom not to fuss about my appearance. Especially when there was nowhere to go and no one to look good for. Was I lacking some crucial evolutionary gene? Did this reflect a lack of self-respect or a higher level of self-acceptance?

Maybe if my mother had allowed me to wear pink it would have been different. When I was a child, redheads didn't wear any shade of red because the color clashed with their hair, or so was the thinking back then. I was denied the girlie hues. Maybe it was because my dear grandma, who lived with my family her entire life, did the ironing and it was nothing I aspired to. Maybe my hippie days were responsible. Was it related to economic class? I could afford to dress nicely, so being unconcerned with my appearance was part of privilege. Or was it one aspect of feminism that I had embraced in my day-to-day living. It irked me that men could get away without primping.

My three pairs of whites were issued on February 1, 1986, the day I was transferred to population, a minimum security area. What a relief that was. The word "minimum" itself sounded so unthreatening. All those tests and the interview before the state and unit classification board must have proved that I was not a dangerous commie plotting to lead a prison uprising. Or maybe they didn't even have all the dirt on me—some felony mischief conviction, sans details, the trial being "apolitical." The fear I held at bay about serving time in a medium or higher security part of population lifted off me. I could do a minimum amount of time, in a minimum area.

The name of my new dorm was un-prison-like. Its name was Reception. It was confusing. The diagnostic unit was my first reception to prison, so what was this other Reception? I found out that the dorm was constructed on the site of what once was the reception area of the Gatesville State School for Boys.

Gatesville was not built to be a women's prison. Its original building was a House of Corrections and Reformatory, opened in 1889 with sixty-eight boys. These were problem boys, unwanted by their communities and families, all under the age of sixteen. Across from the main Gatesville compound, there is a small cemetery where sixteen boys who died in custody in the early 1900s were buried side by side. One of the first things I learned when I entered Reception was that it was haunted by the ghosts of these boys. No one quite knew how they died.

Under the Texas Youth Counsel, and later the Texas Juvenile Justice Department, additional buildings named Hackberry, Riverside, and Valley View were added to provide different levels of supervision for the boys confined to Gatesville. At its height, the complex housed up to 1,500 young men considered to be chronic juvenile delinquents. Through the years, many of the names, if not buildings, were recycled when Gatesville became a women's prison and reflected similar divisions in population.

A few buildings from the original House of Corrections were still in use. That area of Gatesville was renamed Hilltop Hall, and housed the warden and administration offices. The insides of the structures were adorned with ornate ceiling tile and moldings. Historic preservation that fails in Houston is somehow alive and well on the "hill" in Gatesville prison. It hadn't occurred to me until I was incarcerated that prisons had an architectural history. The fact that someone, some authority, recognized the significance of those buildings, which were rehabbed and remained on the Gatesville campus, was impressive. Or maybe it was just cheaper than replacing them.

Gatesville State School for Boys, as it was later named, was closed in the late 1970s after the class action lawsuit, *Morales vs. Turman*. It came to light that the school was in fact being used as a punitive institution for children and violated the 8th Amendment of the US Constitution, citing "cruel and unusual punishment." Hanging boys by their wrists from the bars on the high windows in the dorms was a frequent punishment. Another part of what was considered cruel punishment was the isolation of Gatesville, making it hard for parents to visit their children. When the school closed, the boys were all moved to smaller state schools, foster and group homes, and residential treatment centers.

When Gatesville became a women's prison, the problem of isolation continued. For me, and for most others, the absolute worst thing about being in prison was being away from my children and husband. I had the advantage of knowing that as soon as he could, Tom would visit and bring the kids. He had a working car and money to do that. Many families of my cellmates didn't. Like the boys that were stranded here in the middle of Texas, they faced great hardships keeping connected to family and home. Those links were what we all lived for.

The Reception dorm I transferred to was the same layout as the one in diagnostic: sleeping bunks, common room, and toilet/shower area. The one exception was that the kitchen and eating area were attached to the living area by a short, enclosed hallway. It was a huge disappointment. No guaranteed time to be outside three times a day, if only for a brief walk. There were more windows. That would have to do.

As a newbie I was assigned a top bunk again, but it was roomier. The kind of overcrowding that hit me at the Harris County Jail was non-existent in Gatesville. I learned this was not always the case.

The Texas Department of Corrections had a history of overcrowding and poor conditions, even by prison standards. In 1971, after being in prison at the Goree unit of TDC for ten years, inmate David Ruiz drafted a civil rights complaint exposing the appalling prison environment and gave it to the Assistant Warden to have it notarized. Instead it was ripped up and Ruiz sent to solitary confinement. Ruiz made another copy of the document and gave it to a lawyer who put it in the hands of U.S. District Judge William Wayne Justice. A class action lawsuit ensued. Four years later a victory for the inmates was won. In his ruling, Judge Justice, which is his true and appropriate name, wrote, "The prison system was so pernicious and the inmate's pain and degradation so extensive, it was incapable of description." TDC was put under federal control and was forced to improve sanitation, overcrowding, and safety. David Ruiz remained in prison until he died, continuing to fight for inmates' rights, as well as writing poetry and drawing.

I had some vague recollections when I came to Houston in the 1970s that there were court cases and prison reform. Little did I know that it would personally affect me in a totally unpredictable way. It was more than winding up in Gatesville.

To avoid overcrowding in the prison system, inmates remained in their local county jails until there was a spot available in prison. This way the prison didn't have more inmates than what the federal government mandated. It made the state look good. The backup created was shifted to county jails across Texas. Throughout the 1980s, inmates like myself experienced severe overcrowding in county jails and extended waits to get into the prison system. Staying longer in Harris County was preferable for me, especially when I was moved to the eight-woman cell, but what I didn't realize at the time was that you couldn't start the process of getting out of prison until you got into prison.

When I first found this out, I was angry and anxious. The time in the county jail contributed to my overall time served, but I wasn't sure if the good time credit would be calculated any differently in prison. I knew my two-year sentence would be reduced, but not by how much. Would someone even notice that I was in jail for two-and-a-half months before I entered the prison system? Processing new inmates could take months. This wouldn't affect those with years to serve, but it could affect the short-timers. Would the slow-turning wheels of justice delay my release?

# Chapter 20
# Friend

The barracks-style quarters in the Reception unit held row upon row of metal bunk beds. The beds were more than a place to sleep. The small area around either the top or bottom bunk defined our personal space. Instead of the tote bags we had in diagnostic, there was a rectangular metal lockbox bolted to the back of the bedframe for all our possessions. We still had our own toilet paper, but in population we had access to a better-stocked commissary than the one at jail. Toilet paper upgraded from the prison-issue kind was available. Offenders who had the money to buy toilet paper, instead of using prison-issue, were the high rollers. The bottom bunks had the added benefit of nightstand desks where the commissary-acquired gooseneck lamps and transistor radios were positioned.

These lower bunks were preferred real estate and went to women with seniority. The floor and desks provided opportunities for interior decorating. A popular pastime at Gatesville was making the space around the bunk homey. The principle way to create hominess was with a crochet hook and yarn. Needles, knitting or otherwise, presented a safety issue, as they said in orientation. This made crochet supplies the one and only craft item available at the commissary. This didn't stop my cellmates from creating everything imaginable from the limited resource.

Large afghans covered beds, small ones covered desks, and double thick ones were used as floor mats. Crocheted pillows came in round, square, triangle, and tootsie roll shapes. Yarn dolls and yarn animals spilled over the bunks. Colorful crocheted coasters made of granny squares personalized our small space.

Yarn color changed from week to week so you might start out with a yellow and pink afghan that had a navy blue bottom. Unless we received a copy of a pattern in the mail, we didn't have access to written instructions. The blend of unplanned color combinations and mix-and-match stitches transformed more traditional crochet pieces into individualized creations.

The first woman I spoke with was in the bunk below me. Her name was Jenny. She had a setup that could have been featured in *Good Housekeeping* magazine. She had been in Reception a year and didn't expect to get out for another twenty months. All the rugs, dolls, pillow covers, and desk ornaments were matching pinks and purples. I learned she set high standards for stiches and patterns to come out consistently and made shrewd trades for the right colors. I kind of liked the mismatch, but Jenny fashioned herself after Martha Stewart—who must have fit right in.

I was eager to get my own crochet hook and yarn as soon as I had access to commissary. I wasn't sure what I would make. I didn't want to create a new home. My desire to make things was a desire to make things. Individualizing my temporary nest was merely a byproduct.

In population we all had job assignments. After arriving in Reception, I hoped it was only a matter of days before I would receive mine. Each day I woke up anticipating the structure my new job would create. Each night I went to bed disappointed.

While waiting for the authorities to tell me what my job assignment was, I was waiting on the crochet supplies, and waiting on getting letters that I was able to receive once I was assigned to population. Waiting, waiting. Trying to remain a patient observer waiting for something to happen.

I liked the idea of being a Margaret Mead in prison. I could observe and report on prison life, not be consumed by it, not be consumed by the waiting. It was a question of being patient, waiting.

Margaret Mead wasn't a patient, uninvolved observer. I was hiding behind that role to distance myself from my experience of loneliness and isolation that was a constant force hovering over me. Margaret Meade was waiting on me to do something besides wait.

The only thing to do, as I forced myself to do at the county jail, was hang out in the common area where the all-powerful TV reigned over the natives and strike up a conversation instead of mentally recording the scene. I sat down and watched TV with the few other women there, geared up to start up a conversation. Why hadn't I been friendlier at meals? It wouldn't help to wait for another Sandra. I needed to find out who was new, what their job assignments were, get the lowdown on something besides crochet supplies from Jenny.

No one was talking. I didn't want to interrupt. Against one wall behind the TV, there was a narrow bookcase. On the top shelf there appeared to be some boxes. I got up, softly pushed one of the chairs to the bookcase, and climbed on top of the seat to explore. There were board games gathering dust on the back of the ledge. I held onto the wall with one arm, and stretched the other arm out and pulled down the box as one woman turned her head slightly to watch. It was a game of Scrabble. Scrabble! Prison was full of surprises.

I was never good at Scrabble. I figured playing with someone in prison couldn't be intimidating. The woman viewing my contortions getting the game down came over. She looked at the box, then at me.

"Want to play a game of Scrabble?" she asked.

"Why not," I said.

Her name was Yolanda.

We began the Scrabble game. I was embarrassingly better than her. I have always been a terrible speller, but this was the first time in my life that I had to consciously play poorly. I didn't want to look smart and win. Yolanda may or may not have gotten the idea that I was faking it. She seemed as glad as I was to have a little company and something to do other than watch TV. We struck up a conversation and put the Scrabble game on hold.

Yolanda was from the Rio Grande Valley. She was thirty-seven, like me. Her face was pockmarked and her teeth crooked. Her breath had an oniony smell. She still had a youthful, pretty look, as long as I concentrated on her large, deep-brown eyes and thick eyebrows. She had been in Reception for two months and worked in the laundry.

She said, "I'm always hooking up with bad news men. When my boyfriend asked me to drive him to the Seven Eleven and wait in the car, I didn't know he was going to rob the place. But I should have known. He was always looking for drug money. Stupid me liked drugs too."

"Sounds like he was a bad influence."

"Tell me about it. I have three kids. My boyfriend is the father of the two youngest. We both got busted; he's in prison too. I pleaded with my mom to keep the kids together, but she could only handle two of them. The oldest is staying with his dad's mother. It kills me that they are separated from each other. It's bad enough I can't be there for them. At least they weren't taken away to foster care."

Tears ran down her face and she gulped and sobbed when talking about her kids.

"I can't keep blaming people. I know it's my fault. I'm a terrible mom. But I love my kids and hate to see them suffer for my mistakes. I don't want them to forget me."

"Yolanda, they will never forget you. You're their mom. We all make mistakes," I said.

"I should be punished, but why should they?"

"I know I am lucky with my husband taking care of my kids. I still worry. I got divorced from their dad when they were little. They see him a lot, but they always get shuffled around. Now with me in prison. I hope they realize how much they are loved," I said.

"You have it good," Yolanda said with a bit of a scowl.

"You're right, I have nothing to complain about."

I was concerned that Yolanda wouldn't identify with me. That didn't stop me from identifying with her. She seemed to base her life on the men she met. Even if she didn't say it, maybe she was protecting her man in some way. It seemed to be so bound up with the stories I heard from the other women in prison. Sandra was the only exception.

It was something that continued to gnaw at me. Did everything I do amount to following men? Did I take the rap for Tom because that's what women do? We both never imagined I'd go to prison for spray painting. It was a badge of honor for me to stand up to the court system and not fear any kind of punishment. Did smug righteousness hide my subservient role?

Yolanda didn't know my story. She saw me as the fortunate one. She was right. We both worried about our kids suffering because of us. Mine had advantages that hers didn't. I felt fortunate and guilty.

# Chapter 21
## Saved

The first weekend in population I was eligible for visits. They could be scheduled only one Saturday or Sunday per week, from 8:00 a.m. until 4:00 p.m. We were allocated eight hours a month with the maximum of four visits. The eight hours were divided into two-hour chunks. You could spread out your visits to once a week or blow all eight hours in a one-day visit.

Houston to Gatesville was about a four-hour drive. I was sure Tom would visit, with or without the kids, but I wondered how many of my friends would make that trip. It didn't stop me from submitting the same visitor list I had from the Harris County Jail as soon as I found out how to do it.

While I was in diagnostic I was not allowed to receive mail. I was allowed to write and send letters but had no idea how long it would take them to reach their destination. Once I moved to Reception, any mail that was sent to me was to be forwarded to my new population address, but I hadn't gotten anything yet. Phone communication was not a regular part of prison life. I didn't remember all the requirements, but I knew it would be months before I was eligible for that acquired privilege. I figured Tom must know I was removed from the county jail, but that was about it. Without the web of letters and easy phone access with family and friends, I was beginning to get that sinking feeling again.

It was my first weekend in Reception. Knowing Tom's resourcefulness and worry, whether for him, me, or the kids, I allowed myself to hope. Hope that he would show up for a visit. Hope he would save me once again.

There was a remote possibility that he had called the prison and found the right person, who gave him the right information about my status. He would stay on hold and not give up. All the stars in the universe would line up and bring Tom and, dare I wish, Tony and Pete, to find their way to Gatesville. Or maybe if my karma was good enough. It would happen if it was meant to be. I conjured up notions that at one time would be embarrassing. None of that mattered with my desperation to see my family. No one came on Saturday. Nothing was meant to be.

After 2:00 p.m. on Sunday, I resigned myself that it was too late to expect a visit. I started to tear up and only then realized how much I clung to that possibility, despite the slim-to-none odds. I would have made a pact with the devil to see Tom, Tony, and Pete. How easy it was for me to embrace the irrational. It was frightening.

I slumped on my bunk, totally bereft. There was no way Tom could make it to Gatesville without any communication with me. I was dreaming up unrealistic expectations. Get a grip on reality.

This would end. I was fortunate. Some women in prison never get visits. In with the good air, out with the bad. It barely registered when I heard a voice say, "Betty, if you don't hurry up, you'll miss your visiting time."

I vaulted to my feet and nearly tripped, following the guard out the Reception hallway to the dining room.

We went out a door, down a short path, to a squat building. This was the first time I was outside since leaving diagnostic.

We entered a large, bright room, not as dungeon-like as in the county. I quickly scanned the area. There were two guards sitting at a table with plastic flowers in a vase. Opposite them was a line of chairs facing a see-through wall. Only one chair was occupied. It took a moment to realize that Tom, Tony, and Pete were already on the other side looking at me. They had huge smiles on their faces, and I couldn't tell who was happiest. As I sat down on a chair facing them, tears of joy and longing took over. Through the round microphone opening in the transparent partition, I repeated and repeated, "I love you all, I love you all so much."

Tom said, "I was on the phone for what seemed like hours trying to find you and see if we could visit. Sorry we are so late, we got here as soon as we could. It's worth it."

"It's unbelievable that you all are here. I have the best family. And Tony and Pete, you are the champions of the world. I am so happy you all are here."

"Thanks, Mom."

"Thanks, Mommy."

I blew Tony and Pete kisses and looked at Tom.

"I hope the drive was not too bad."

"It's a pain, I have to admit. We played thirty questions a hundred times in the car."

"And I won," said Tony.

"I won too" said Peter.

Hearing my kids banter had me crying some more.

"I have a friend from my dharma group who lives in Austin, so we will spend the night there," said Tom. "We'll have some fun and get some tacos, right, kids?"

"Yes!" they both squealed.

"I just feel bad I couldn't get us out here any earlier."

"Seeing you here, actually here, in person, means so much. I still can't believe my eyes."

"I'd do anything to see you."

A guard announced it was five minutes to 4:00 p.m. and time to say goodbye. It felt like we were still saying hello. But it didn't matter. Seeing my family would sustain me for another week. In the five minutes before he left, Tom assured me that he had received my letters, that he gave out my new address to our friends, that he spoke to my dad regularly and that I would have a visit by someone every weekend.

On the way back to my dorm after the visit, I tried to stop the crying that had started again. I didn't think there were any tears left in me. I was a wreck. As I reached my bunk, women I didn't even know gave me hugs and assured me that when they saw their kids for the first time in the prison visiting area, it broke them up too.

That night I thought about the visit. Tom was so dedicated. He was a better stepdad than anyone could believe. It was good that the first visit was short. Enough for the kids to take all this in without it be overwhelming. Tony and Pete would get through this. With visits on the weekends I'd have something to look forward to. The weeks would turn into months. The months would pass, how many more in Gatesville I didn't know. All I knew was I had Tony, Pete, and Tom, my anchors, my loves.

# Chapter 22
# Not Saved

The second Sunday morning in Reception, Yolanda showed up at my bunk with a big, closed-mouth smile on her face. She had mastered the art of smiling, talking, and eating without exposing her teeth.

"Wanna go to church service with me?" she asked.

I hesitated, cleared my throat, and said, "I'm kind of Jewish."

"What does that mean?"

"Ah, well, it's hard to explain."

Yolanda stared at me. I'm sure my body language said, *please don't ask me anymore.* Yolanda took the cue and responded, "You could come with me to church just to get out of here."

"I'll think about it."

This Jewish thing was difficult for me. I didn't want to be a nothing in prison, but felt that saying I was Jewish would imply an allegiance to religion. With a last name of Sullivan and red hair, people assumed I was Irish. The subtleties of my coarse, frizzy hair texture, and my "Roman" nose, as my mother politely called it, didn't betray my ethnicity in Texas. The assumption was that everyone was Christian. Maybe if I had horns. I couldn't blame them; growing up on Long Island, I assumed everyone was Jewish.

In the 1950s neighborhood where I grew up, Yiddish-speaking grandparents and knowing someone who died in the Holocaust were the norms. I never knew until I left home that Goldstein and Greenberg were identified as Jewish names. My brain knew that Jews were a minority, but my experience said they were all over the place.

My family belonged to a synagogue and my brother had a Bar Mitzvah. A Bat Mitzvah, the female equivalent, was not a high priority for girls back then and was a low priority for me. I lost interest in Sunday school early on and the thought of studying Hebrew was horrifying. Languages, even English, were my worst subjects in school. Plus my parents were not the type to push.

Religion for the Baers meant financial support of the synagogue and showing up at the most once a year, for Yom Kippur. Our Jewish practice was sharing gefilte fish, stuffed derma, matzah ball soup, and honey cake at the appropriate Jewish holiday meals. Grownups hotly debated world affairs, not the Torah.

When I once asked my mother if there was a god, she said, "If you believe in one, then there is." That sounded reasonable to me. My dad, on the other hand, once said, "Religion is the opiate of the masses." I could never figure out how Marx poached that phrase from him.

I gathered that my Dad associated religion with his parents' Eastern European, old-country, boiled, tasteless chicken and restricted lifestyle. My father was a modern man. Tradition was part of his identity, only in small doses. He described himself as an "atheist Jew," which, in truth, is not an oxymoron.

As a communist I had no problem dismissing religion. I thought it was all fabricated and had no comprehension of how anyone could seriously believe in God. Religion was another way for the capitalists to deceive people, by promoting a better life in the hereafter. Hypocrisy defined religious leaders who waged war in the name of religious righteousness. That religion predated Capitalism and that, for many, religious beliefs were a moral guide and intertwined with social justice were of no irrelevance. It was a simple matter: religion bad, Marxist dialectical materialism good. The idea that religion, like politics, can be utilized in positive and negative ways was beyond me, at that time.

Church is a big draw in prison. Talk about a captive audience. When Yolanda first asked me along, my worldview was becoming more inclusive—but going to a religious service, a church, of all places, was worrisome. Despite my secular Jewish roots, the unspoken message I received from my parents, however one receives that sort of thing, was that Christians still had a grudge against Jews, because "we" had killed Jesus.

Then I thought, *what have I got to lose?* I had gotten comfortable with calling myself an agnostic. It gave me permission to be indecisive about the spiritual realm. "Living in the Mystery" had an attractive ring to it.

There were powerful things out there that I hadn't figured out. There were forces that kept us connected that I didn't understand. Maybe that was God for some people. Or what they meant when they spoke about the spiritual. Or their essence. Or what would become of that part of them after they died. I hoped that when I died, if there was anything that carried on beyond what people remembered of me, I wouldn't be denied it because of my doubt. Or dying could be the ultimate connectedness, no self to keep us separate.

I decided to go to church with Yolanda because of Yolanda and Margaret Mead. I spent too much of my life trying to change people's beliefs instead of trying to understand what they believed. Yolanda said there would be music at the church service. One of my favorite singers, Aretha Franklin, had deep roots in gospel music. Maybe I could use some of my years of piano lessons and tickle the ivories by accompanying a soulful gospel choir in prison.

The Sunday sermon started at 9:00 a.m. I got spruced up in my best visitor whites and make up, per Yolanda's instructions. We lined up deuced, and walked along with the group from our dorm to a small, white building that served as a chapel on Sundays. The February morning was chilly and refreshing. I had missed breathing in the country air and crunching the paths on the way to meals while I was in diagnostic, and I resolved to find a way to get outside more. We arrived at our destination, filed in, and sat down on the folding chairs laid out in neat rows, our hands in our laps like obedient school girls.

The wiggly cracks on the wall plaster and thick window molding looped around the room. This was one of the historic buildings that had not been remodeled. "If these walls could talk" hit me as a profound cliché.

A bald man stood behind a wooden podium set up in front of the chairs. He introduced himself.

"Good morning, ladies. I welcome you, one and all. A special welcome for those of you who have not been here before. I'm Deacon Burns from the Riverside Baptist Church in the city of Gatesville. We have been operating outreach prison ministries for many years. I'm here today to share God's word with you.

"Sisters, Jesus is by your side. If you accept Jesus as your savior you will never walk alone."

"Hallelujah!"

"Sisters, whatever you did that got you into prison, it will not, I say, will not, keep you from Heaven as long as you accept Jesus Christ as your savior."

"Hallelujah!"

"Sisters, Jesus died for your sins and will await you with open arms on judgment day."

"Hallelujah, Hallelujah!"

The offenders rose up and sat down for each Hallelujah. I stood too. It was like standing for the national anthem at a baseball game. Not standing was embarrassing, even if I wasn't all-in.

"Sisters, God loves you, never forget that!"

"Do you feel God's love?

"Can you feel the presence of the Lord right now?"

"Thank you, Jesus! Thank you, Jesus!" rang out. Joyful shouting and clapping erupted at the deacon's every word.

Jesus's name was called more and more. I eyed the door several times, but there was no way I could sneak out. Yolanda nudged me with her elbow.

Deacon Burns looked at his watch and rested his hands on the podium and said: "Amen."

A chorus of amens flowed from the women as they found their seats and sat down. I said, "Thank God," to myself too.

The deacon looked to the back of the room. A member of the outreach ministry sitting in the last row of chairs caught his gaze. Deacon Burns gave a nod. The woman got up from her seat and passed out Christian literature and prayer request forms to the offenders. I was feeling more and more like an outsider. I didn't want any of it, but it seemed impolite to refuse the offering. Maybe there was someone back at the dorm I could give the prayer requests to. I hated wasting paper. Then I thought, *me handing out prayer requests, what had I gotten myself into?*

Deacon Burns said, "I'd like everyone to place the materials on your seat, stand up one more time, and take hold of your neighbor's hand."

Yolanda squeezed my hand. After Deacon Burns sang the first note of "Amazing Grace," the rest of the group joined in.

I studied the ladies in the room. They were arm-in-arm, eyes glistening, their faces aglow. Their singing was beautiful. I sensed a genuine feeling of happiness and relief. I hummed along and swayed to the music. The balm of togetherness smoothed my judgmental edges. This is why people go to church. It was hope. It was love. We were one with God, ourselves, everyone. I got it. I wanted it. Until I looked up. For Sunday service, a crucifix hung on the back wall. There was Jesus nailed to the cross, looking down. At me. The spell broke. Suddenly I felt more Jewish than I had in my entire life. Church let out, and I never went back.

*Feb. 6, 1986*
*My Dear Daughter, Betty,*

*You mentioned you went to church service. I recall when I was in Germany perhaps one or two hundred yards from the line and it was quiet and I heard a frequent call for services (Catholic). It was cold and I could not warm up. I thought that the services were held in a place warmer than the great outdoors. I went over. It was a little shelter (I can't recall all the details) and I found myself partially indoors and partially outdoors. I listened, half my body was cold and I considered that to stay was not worth the effort.*

*My officers knew I was Jewish, so did everyone else. They were amused and somewhat confused and interested since they never knew a Jew in their life. The three officers, one who was the assistant company commander, all lieutenants, had a feeling that if I was close by that I was a touchstone of life. One of them insisted that we have a double foxhole and I could not shake him until I selected a foxhole that was too small for the two of us.*

*My experience with chaplains in the Army is as follows. After induction, clothing, shots, and KP in Camp Upton, we were put in a troop train to Camp Blanding, Florida, about 30 miles or more inland from Jacksonville. The chaplain made a moving speech and it sounded like a rabbi's blessing combined with a funeral oration. We were only going for training; however, we had God's blessings. It was a good, strong blessing and speech, and I was impressed with the chaplain.*

*In France and Germany the chaplain had his jeep with the battalion aid station, which consisted of doctors plus some enlisted men who were medics and litter bearers. Litter bearers brought in the wounded, the dead were collected in trucks and piled like firewood after the front moved three to five miles. The chaplain was three to five to ten miles behind the lines. When we went to a so-called rest area, to wash, clean, change clothes, etc., we were near the battalion aid station and the chaplain. I took some time to see what sort of chap the chaplain was, and no doubt, he was Catholic. He appeared hard boiled, never a smile on his face, and the impression I got was that he suspected the soldiers would use him if given the opportunity. All sermons were controlled by the Army. The chaplain was instructed to remind the soldiers to obey their officers, etc.*

*I gather that the prison chaplain not paid by the State of Texas would be in a different position, but I doubt whether he would go out of his way to find you. If he does, he will have nothing to offer.*

*Love, Dad*

# Chapter 23
# Waiting and What It's Worth

The prison commissary was stocked with yellow legal notepads. It was the first thing I bought. The lined paper was used as stationary and the cardboard back of the pad became my homemade calendar. As I had in jail, I X-ed off each day. In addition I used the calendar to keep track of the letters I received every day and checked off when I responded. It was my longhand Excel spreadsheet. Letters I sent from prison had more and more Margaret Meade to them. I wrote about the surrounding country vistas, the farm-to-table environment, the historic buildings, and meeting women from all parts of the state. I emphasized being strong, making friends, while I felt disconnected and shy and didn't let on that I cried myself to sleep.

The envelopes available from the commissary had the postage embossed, as there was no way to buy stamps. It all looked utilitarian until I noticed my downstairs bunkmate, Jenny, had envelopes decorated with tattoo-like roses. The petals were pink and the leaves green. They were handmade, but we had no access to colored pencils, color pens, or crayons. I wondered how Jenny did it.

One day she let me watch. To make the red rose coloring, the source was wooden matches from the commissary that all the smokers had. You placed the match head in your mouth, swirled your tongue around it, and when it was good and slimy, red "paint" appeared.

The matchstick was used as the paint brush. If it dried up, a few more drops of saliva loosed the red from the phosphorous tip, producing more paint. For the green leaves, you'd gently lick green M&Ms to turn the colored coating into a liquid-y state, smear some on the tip of your finger, and fill between the ink lines. The bonus was all those extra M&Ms devoid of their food coloring were just as tasty to pop in your mouth as you painted away.

Jenny knew all about prison crafts. She said that soap carving was popular in the men's prison. She told me they used shoe polish to paint the soap black, which means they must have had shoes while we had sneakers. Without access to knives, she had no idea what they carved with. These soap sculptures were the main craft with men. Many were made to look like small guns. Some looked real enough to pass for weapons and got the male prisoners in trouble.

Decorating all my envelopes became a creative outlet. It was a way to send off letters with a flourish.

At last I received my crochet supplies. Trouble was I didn't know how to crochet. My mother and her friends were knitters. None of them were interested in crochet. The history of knitting goes back way before crocheting, although it's hard to think of my Mom as a yarn snob. Regardless, I only learned to knit. Jenny let me watch her wield the single crochet hook and yarn, and before long I was making chains of stiches. Crocheting was suited to making afghans. Before I tackled an afghan, I practiced by making a pull-string bag of as many colors and stiches as I could. It was a success.

I got busy on an afghan for a wedding present for Tom's brother, Phil, and his soon-to-be wife, Roseanne.

Tom's family, like mine, was entirely supportive of me in prison. Roseanne and Phil postponed their wedding until I got out of prison and could be there. In retrospect it seems peculiar giving a prison-crafted afghan for a wedding gift. I wouldn't want a memento from prison. I remember ripping out rows of crochet stitching that weren't perfect, being compelled to complete a faultless present. Maybe I got so wrapped up in the repetitive cycle of hooking the yarn that the thought of how the afghan would be received didn't cross my mind.

Tom sent me a black and white professional photo of Tony and Pete. A photographer who became interested in my case had taken pictures of the kids. They were stunning. I wrapped yarn around a cutout piece of cardboard from another legal pad to make a frame for the picture. That cardboard- and yarn-framed picture was the ultimate treasured possession at my bedside.

I was beginning to congratulate myself on being the most creative prisoner until I found out that many of the offenders wrote poetry. I was surprised at first. Poetry seemed to appeal to a more literary crowd than the ones reading romance novels. In the one letter I received from Sandra, after her transfer to medium security population, she included a poem that one of her new dorm mates wrote. It was passed around Gatesville, included in letters.

*Doin' Time*

*I'm not really guilty*
*Just a victim of the times.*
*What satisfied my body*
*Never satisfied my mind*

*I walked through life not knowing*
*Just where to draw the line.*
*It's easy making your own hell*
*But heaven's hard to find.*

*Amen, Lisa Brown*

Poetry poured from our wounds and mended them too. I learned that reading poetry was common. It wasn't only me who was needy, anxious, and didn't know how much to keep in or let out. The other women, as well-adjusted as they acted, concealed their suffering too. I asked for and received poems through the mail. Tom would hand-copy a poem of Marge Piercy's or Walt Whitman's and enclose it with his letter to me. Jack, in response to my letter about the first few days of diagnostic, sent me a poem of his own.

*Sunday,     the*
*morning is cold and wet*
*frost glazes my window eyes*
*over*
*You are sleeping     still*
*somewhere far*
*or maybe looking into the mirror*
*    just breathing*

*but I am unaware, alone   distant*
*sitting in the cool grey nothing*
*on Edward Hopper light*
*Slants dim, shines through small window*

*and as I touch the light,    a shaft*
*I shudder*
*with a thin frost,    crystalline*
*embrace,    covered frozen*
*motionless*

    *I feel you move somewhere*
    *understanding now with sudden shiver*
    *we are together every moment anyway*

*Having no wings to fly*
*I kiss the cool air*
*Knowing it's the same*
*you breathe        you will breathe*

    I never appreciated poetry more than when I was in prison. This improbable thing I shared with the women I lived with. Not so improbable, poetry is not for people in a hurry; we weren't going anywhere. Except for the places where poetry could take us.

# Chapter 24
# Job

Days wore on in Reception. With no set schedule, no recreation, and plenty of M&Ms, my new prison whites were feeling a bit tight. You might think getting fat would be the last thing to be worried about in prison, but I was beginning to feel like gaining weight was part of losing control. I needed every bit of control I could find. The fear of losing my embryo of self terrified me. Yolanda had her job assignment. No one new transferred to Reception. I was the only one left untethered. That changed without warning.

At 2:45 a.m. a guard came into the dorm, woke me up, and told me to get dressed for my 3:00-10:00 a.m. breakfast work shift in the kitchen. The guard roused the rest of the women on my shift after the visit to my bunk, an event I slept through every other night.

Still shaking off sleep, the seven of us lined up at the doorway leading out of the dorm at 2:55 a.m. We filed into the hallway separating the dorm and kitchen where everyone stopped. The guard went down the line, frisking us before opening the kitchen door and leading us inside.

We were deposited in the back of the kitchen. The wall was lined with cubbies holding large, white aprons and kerchiefs. Following the others, I grabbed an apron and tied it behind my back, wrapped the kerchief around my head, and walked into the main kitchen area feeling like I was cast as a peasant in *Fiddler on the Roof.*

On one long wall across from the scratched up prep table were enormous hooks with equally massive pots and pans. In the corner was a locked cabinet for the knives. Each knife had TDC branded onto its wooden handle and was accounted for before and after every shift on the silhouette pegboard where it hung. The yeast was in a separate, locked compartment, measured and tracked as well, to prevent us from stealing it and making hooch.

My job involved neither knives nor yeast. I was a dishwasher, but didn't use the dishwasher. Putting dishes in the dishwasher was the next job up, and I was the bottom of the barrel, cleaning industrial-sized skillets, assorted pans, cookie sheets, and mixing bowls. Whatever didn't fit in the dishwasher, which looked as if it could have held the kitchen sink, was up to me to clean.

While the cooks cooked, I rubbed and rinsed, scurrying to keep from getting behind, soap bubbles airborne and water splashing, drying rags slapping the wet pots. A revolving wheel of washing, drying, and more washing, I was running in circles in another kind of gerbil cage.

Once breakfast was ready, the kitchen crew gorged on their fill, standing up at the prep area. My hands turned red and ragged and I took a moment to run back to the cubby area to see if there were any rubber gloves. There were none. Asking someone about gloves crossed my mind, but I didn't want them to think I was a wimp. After eating we regrouped behind the steam table to serve the women in Reception as they showed up in an orderly procession at 4:30 a.m. for official breakfast in the dining room off the kitchen.

When breakfast was done, whatever was leftover was thrown in buckets where it was renamed slop. I cleaned the rectangular pans and covers from the steam table as the cooks prepped for lunch. Towards the end of the shift, I took out the trashcans and buckets. I shoveled the slop into larger vats for pigs raised on the prison farm to feast on. The kitchen lunch shift came in to take our places. Leaving the kitchen we all got frisked again.

After my shift I took a hot shower and conked out in bed, holding a pillow tight over my ears, and fitfully slept until suppertime. The dorm was close to empty during the day and the pillow was as much to cover my teary eyes as to block out noise. As relieved as I was to get a job, I became so worried about getting enough sleep that it kept me awake.

Before my arrest, when I was still married to Joe, I got a job as a mail handler on the night shift at the post office on Franklin Street in Houston. After getting home I fixed breakfast for Tony and Pete and got them ready for Joe to drop them off at child care. He did this on his way to work at U.S. Steel, which was at one time located outside of Baytown. Once the house was empty and silent, I had a beer and went to sleep. Sleeping during the day was something my body fought. I didn't get used to sleeping during the day, but it had its advantages. I was getting by on less sleep than I ever dreamed possible, and I could pick the kids up from child care earlier than most working parents.

Adjusting to the early morning prison shift never happened. It seemed my internal clock was not going to reset to the external conditions, despite spending hours upon hours lying on my bunk, willing sleep to come. The missing link was a beer. I hadn't comprehended how essential it was.

After a week and a half of diligent scrubbing and drying, aching arms, and red chapped hands, a new offender was put on pots and pans and I moved up to dishwasher and setting up trays for segregation. Segregation or "seg," was a blanket term that we used. The prison lingo was more complex.

The most common segregation was solitary confinement. Offenders were put there for disciplinary punishment. Solitary confinement was limited to fifteen-day sentences—not that you were guaranteed to get out after fifteen days. Consecutive sentences were frequent. In that case seventy hours were required between these sentences and were spent in administrative segregation.

Administrative segregation housed offenders who were at risk for being harmed by other offenders. This could mean a snitch, a gang member, or a child molester. Although women's prison wasn't known for violent gangs and child molesters, when rumors surfaced about an offender being imprisoned for harming a child, she was shunned. There was one woman in my dorm accused of killing her child. It was taboo to speak to this woman. This was the first rule made by offenders, not prison officials. Besides her, I didn't think anyone in our dorm could be a candidate for segregation. I figured that as a minimum-security dorm, we were deemed the least likely to know someone in seg and therefore entrusted the task to fix their trays without worry of sneaking anything along the way.

The seg trays were hard, tan, plastic rectangles with divided serving sections. There were no dishes; the food went directly on the tray. The only utensil was a spoon. One day, as I was setting up the trays, Connie, who was one of the cooks, stomped over from the stove and caught my hand.

"What are you doing putting those fine biscuits on that tray?" she asked.

"They're just biscuits," I said. "I thought that was what I was supposed to be doing."

"Burnt biscuits go on there."

"Don't those go out to the pigs?"

"That shows what you know. First, they are hogs. Second, if you wound up in seg, you're a hog anyway."

Connie was a well-respected cook who kept "her" kitchen running smoothly. I didn't want to get on her bad side.

"These were just the first biscuits I saw."

"Hum," she said. "Here, take this burnt bacon then." She slammed a plate of charred bacon down and marched off.

As I finished up the seg trays with burnt bacon, it struck me as unfair. Connie was intentionally putting the worst food on the seg trays. There was plenty of good food and with the pigs, or hogs, nothing was wasted. Still I did as Connie said.

That morning when I tried to sleep, my stomach started making gurgling sounds as I thought about the women in segregation. Did "all for one and one for all" stop there? They were isolated all day. Even the food said "you're worthless." Every one of them couldn't be a hog or a pig. Then there was that woman who harmed her child. I wasn't sure about that. Wouldn't she already be destroyed inside? What about truly evil people? Or was that term another way to disassociate one from another? Should compassion be universal? Was Mother Theresa, not Mao, becoming my role model?

Connie was in my dorm and part of a clique of black women who stayed to themselves. I didn't want to have any problems with Connie, but I didn't like being pushed around by her, either. I wanted to defend the defenseless. I wanted to stand up for myself. I wanted to know what the difference between a hog and a pig was too.

Yolanda bought a pocket dictionary from commissary, being inspired by our scrabble games. I went over to her bunk and asked her to look up pigs and hogs for me.

"Why do you care about that?"

"It's just some of the women say we have pigs on the prison farm and some say hogs." I didn't want to draw her into my dealings with Connie or have to hear that she thought Connie was right.

"OK, let's see. It says pigs and hogs are both swine. Pigs are younger and hogs are older. I bet they're both out there."

So we both were right. That night the women in seg entered my dreams. They seemed nice enough in a ghoulish way. Maybe it was true that Gatesville was haunted. One of the apparitions whispered that she couldn't help it, she had a short fuse, and regretted getting into trouble. Another said she sure would appreciate someone treating her like a person and not a mental case. I wanted to trust those spirits, but I didn't want to be deceived by them, either. I decided I'd rather be sympathetic and wrong then heartless and right.

The following morning I fixed the seg trays with regular bacon, eggs, and biscuits. I kept my head down, thinking that if I didn't look at Connie then she wouldn't see me.

She came over, faster than last time.

"What the hell are you doing?"

"I'm just setting up the seg trays," I said, smiling innocently enough.

"Look, I told you that the worst food goes on the seg trays. That's the way we do it here. If you can't do it that way, then I'll get someone else to do it right."

Connie shot up her hands and huffed away before I could answer. Not that I had an answer.

Besides a false sense of confidence that I could deal with a graveyard shift, the post office offered me the experience of being in the minority. Federal employment with good benefits was a plum job for anyone with a high school diploma. The entrance test attracted a majority of young black people.

I never felt like I was much of a political organizer at the post office. The radical movement in this country had passed and the liberation struggles in the rest of the world had quieted down. As much as the government was my enemy, I couldn't help notice that the U.S. Postal Service was inclusive of minorities, had a strong union, and provided a decent salary. As a white person I could hardly preach about the injustice of racism. Although the work itself was not mentally challenging, the general feeling was that it was a job worth sticking with. My coworkers created an environment where the work got done with more good times than grumbling. Laughter and friendly chatter made the time go by as the mail got sorted.

As open-minded as I viewed myself and as much as I assumed that my coworkers shared, whether they expressed it or not, a distrust of the powers that be, I felt acutely self-conscious. Beside the racial divide, I was keenly aware that working towards retirement at the post office was not in my future. I was planted in the post office to carry out a political agenda first, to make a living second. I still believed it was a worthy cause, but found myself "forgetting" to bring to work those *Revolutionary Worker* newspapers that I could share or even sell (!) to my coworkers at lunch break.

With Connie and her crew, it was more complicated. Along with being coworkers, we were cohabiters. It was more important for me to be accepted than to make a political point. I didn't know what I was, didn't know what I believed, but didn't want to come across as some bleeding-heart, white liberal. That didn't take away my objection to trashing the women in seg, whoever they were and whatever they did. Putting others down to bring us up. That was what I objected to. The solidarity I experienced among the women in prison and jail was one of the things that made it bearable.

The two days off from work couldn't come fast enough. I had mail to answer and envelopes to decorate. But mostly I wanted distance from Connie's watch. If our differences escalated, I knew I would back down. She would win.

My second day off I approached Yolanda. "Do you know anyone who was sent to seg?"

"Does this have something to do with pigs and hogs?" she asked. "You've been acting real funny lately."

"Honestly, Yolanda, it's about the trays I set up for them. It's not a big deal, but I wonder just how much different they are from the rest of us."

"I don't know anyone in segregation. I think it's the maximum-security dorms that have those problems. I heard of one woman who got sent to segregation because she was saying she was sick and wouldn't work and the doctors said she could work. After so much back and forth, they hauled her off," she said.

"That's awful," I said.

"She could have been trying to get out of work, you don't know. There are plenty of bad people in here."

"Guess I don't like to think about that," I said.

"No offense," Yolanda said. "But this is prison. Not everyone is stupid like me. Some of them like to cause trouble. Some are just plain bad. There have to be rules."

"It's just that I don't see that putting the worst food on the seg trays helps anything. That's not a prison rule, right? This sounds like an excuse, but maybe some of those women never had anything but bad treatment, and who are we to judge?"

"All I know is that Connie is doing things the way they always get done. If someone gets thrown into seg, there's nothing you can do about it. You can think of people as victims, but they still have a mind of their own."

I knew Yolanda had a point, plus she was making me feel better and giving me a way out. Why did I think there weren't bad people out there who got what they deserved? Did I fail to grow up from the Pollyanna I was in high school? But I still didn't want to be that cynical person. This is the way it is. People get what they deserve. Get real.

Was there some basic human dignity we had in common or would there always be *us* and *them*? As long as They had it worse than We did, it made Us feel better. Us against them was cropping up more and more in prison as our environment and personal lives became routine and stable. Space grew between us and camaraderie eroded into sub groups based on ethnicity and who liked whom. And if I really thought compassion-for-all was the answer, what about those with power?

I went back to work in the kitchen the next day, or night, whatever you call 2:45 a.m. I took my place at the dishwasher, suited up in apron and kerchief, ready to roll up my sleeves if my prison whites had long sleeves. After the first set of dishes were loaded, I poured in the detergent, turned on the roaring machine, then walked up to Connie as she was kneading bread and said, "Hi."

She didn't look up. I slipped off to fix the seg trays. If I saw something a teeny bit burnt, I'd put in on the tray, but I didn't examine the food. Most everything inedible made its way into the slop bucket before it got to the prep areas anyway.

I looked over my shoulder from time to time. Connie was still kneading dough and ignoring me. It didn't seem like she wanted to make this seg tray a big issue after all. The days off could have given her time to dismiss me and my foolishness. I'd think of it as unspoken detente. We could be on the same side after all, making it another day in prison.

# Chapter 25
# Spring

My life shrank. Between the kitchen, the dorm, and my little bunk space, it wasn't openly claustrophobic, but subconsciously crippling. There was just enough space to keep me on edge without going over the edge. Greys and browns were the only colors visible from our dorm windows. There was no outside, not even a rooftop. It was calculated. I was an object, watched and evaluated by guards and the other offenders. I shifted between this paranoid state and an out-of-body state— floating around, walking around the bunks, checking out the latest in crochet creations, catching a show on TV. Everyone slept at different times according to their work schedule. Getting up at 2:30 a.m. made for a surreal element of timelessness.

Change came at the end of March. In Houston the invigorating, temperate winter mutates into oven-hot and steamy. In Gatesville springtime was an actual season. Even behind bars I sensed an awakening. The ground started greening. Black V formations of migrating birds took over the sky. The steel bars on the window disappeared when I spied a young wobbly colt snuggling up to its mother mare in the distance. June bugs invaded the hallways connecting the dorm to the kitchen. Those tiny intersections of nature were like a walk in the woods.

Springtime brought a new job: working in the guard's kitchen as a short order cook. The hours were the same, but the pace was slower. The coffee was made in a people-sized coffee maker not an industrial vat that required dragging across the room to clean. I conquered sunny side up eggs made on a cast-iron griddle. The perfect yokes were not too runny or overcooked. My free-world self only made scrambled eggs for fear of stiff, orange centers. Maybe this could be considered job training.

Except that it was weird cooking for the guards. A house slave. Part of me flinched at the idea that the prison establishment trusted me to cook for the staff—not that they shouldn't. I did my job. I didn't grovel, I didn't snitch, I didn't curry favor with the guards. I avoided them more than anything. I was acquiring "good time" credit. There was no shame in being a model offender, or so I reminded myself.

The best thing was that Connie was out of the picture. Every day in the Reception kitchen was clouded with a possible breach of our détente over the seg trays. Fortunately nothing much got burnt. I didn't realize until the job transfer how tense it was below the surface. With the new job and with spring's arrival, my calendar was filling up with Xs as time ticked by.

Enlivened by the mild, sparkling daylight, one of the guards, Ms. Nelson, put up a volleyball net in a grassy square outside our dorm. She organized volleyball games Tuesdays and Thursdays at 3:00 p.m., a time between most work and sleep shifts. Despite being short I loved playing volleyball. I was quick and could whack the ball hard with my forearm serve, a surprise to my teammates. Being good at volleyball gave me a feeling of competency, something I rarely felt in prison. The chance to be outdoors and engage with my cellmates, with a sense of confidence, made me a regular at volleyball.

One afternoon Jenny came out to play. As she walked past me, she rubbed her eyes with her fists. She found a place on the back row of the opposite side of the net, her spine hunched over and her shoulders drooping. I was up to serve and gave the volleyball a hard punch. The ball arched through the air and came down in front of Jenny. She took a step back and let it drop and bounce to a stop. She bent down and rolled it back under the net. A point for us.

I threw the ball up in the air and hit another serve in her direction. She moved to the side and watched the ball fall out of the air. Untouched. My team scored again.

It didn't seem fair to take advantage of her weakness. But sports are about winning. All's fair in love and war—and sports? My teammates looked at me with big grins. A surge of competition, generally not my nature, gushed through me. My chance to be the hero. One more serve to Jenny. She raised up her hand, which grazed the ball, then the ball went far out of bounds. If she had let that one go, the serve would have changed hands. Jenny's teammates started muttering.

I remembered one of my favorite sayings from Mao: "Friendship first, competition second." It was one of those slogans I repeated to folks who referred to Mao as a monster. How can you despise a man who comes up with such a sympathetic homily? I threw up the ball once more and hit it hard and as far away from Jenny as I could. Another woman on Jenny's side returned it. We had a rousing volley going. I dove like mad to keep the ball in play when it came back to me, but it slipped through my fingers. We lost the point. Jenny gave me a half-smile. My heart felt a pang of compassion.

Jenny left the game, and plunked down on the grass as I continued to play. Ms. Nelson materialized and walked over to where Jenny was sitting. I kept looking their way and paying attention to the game as best I could. Ms. Nelson kneeled down on one knee next to Jenny's folded body and fed her a tissue. Jenny blew her nose and wiped her eyes while Ms. Nelson gently patted her on the back. They looked so in-tune. Just a few minutes earlier, I was feeling virtuous for forfeiting volleyball points in the name of "Friendship First." Now this prison guard, one of "Them," looked like she was Jenny's best friend.

Guards. They were officially called correction officers (CO). In orientation we were told when addressing the CO to use the title "Ms." along with the last name on the metal badge they wore on the chest pocket of their uniform. Either feminist phrasing reached Gatesville or they were concealing their marital status. The COs addressed us by our first names. Yet when they asked us a question, or gave a verbal order, the proper response was "Yes, Ma'am" or "No, Ma'am." For the offenders native to Texas, this was natural. To me all this Ma'am-ing sounded like a throwback to plantation lingo.

Ms. Nelson was one of the younger guards. With the absence of wrinkles and her bouncy ponytail, she looked like a teenager. She must have been in her twenties. She wore her uniform cinched tightly at the waist and smiled and chatted with the offenders as her ponytail bobbed. The other guards, by comparison, looked like firmly stuffed soldiers.

The guards' eating area had several faux-wood, round tables with peg-backed chairs. Short, gingham fabric hung over the windows. These curtains barely camouflaged the bars. The guards rotated in for breakfast, not deuced like the offenders. They placed their breakfast order with me then turned and took seats alone, while I cooked. And then there was Ms. Nelson. She walked into the dining area as if we were all one big, happy family.

"Betty, can you please put just half a biscuit on my tray? If you put a whole one on there, I'll never be able to restrain myself from eating it."

"Yes, Ma'am."

"Next to chocolate, these biscuits are the best thing I've ever eaten," she said.

I was thinking the exact same thing. Ms. Nelson started conversations with me every morning.

"There's nothing like the smell of bacon," she said. "Even if it isn't the best thing for you, I have to indulge every once in a while."

"Yes, Ma'am. They're a real temptation."

"You got that right," she said. "The other COs hound me to eat more. They say I'm so skinny it wouldn't make a difference. But I'm only this weight because I watch what I eat. I don't want to turn into a biscuit myself."

"I know what you mean. I don't want to come home from prison looking like one of those hogs we fatten up."

"Ha, you don't have to worry about that."

"But I worry that if I don't worry, that's when my discipline will break down."

"We've got that in common," she said.

Another morning Ms. Nelson came in towards the end of my breakfast shift.

"Hi Betty, any idea how fresh the coffee is?"

I went over to the coffee maker and noticed that what was left in the pot looked dreary and dark. I dumped it out and raised my voice so that Ms. Nelson could hear. "I'm making a new pot right now, Ma'm." After measuring the grounds and water the coffee machine started grunting. I came back to the counter where Ms. Nelson was still standing.

"Thanks a lot," she said. "I appreciate you making fresh coffee."

"You're welcome, Ma'am."

Ms. Nelson rested her forearm on the counter while the coffee brewed. We both drew in the tantalizing aroma.

"You know, I've worked here for three years and feel a lot of sympathy for y'all. I grew up just down the road in Waco. Most of my family works in the prison system. I never wanted to follow in their footsteps. Then my brother found his way onto the wrong side of the law. I thought about being a social worker so that I could help people before they wound up in a place like this. I couldn't believe how much school and debt was involved. I couldn't handle it. To be a CO, all I needed was a high school diploma. Plus I got a recruitment bonus. I think if I can show some concern for the ladies here, it's doing the same thing."

"I saw you with Jenny the other day at the volleyball game. That night she said you spending time with her really helped."

"That makes me feel good. I know some of the COs worry about being taken advantage of. Believe me it happens. But being in this minimum-security area, I've found that if I show a little heart it can go a long way. If you are with the same people year after year it creates a bond. I know it's a world of difference; we get off work and go home. I can't help but think that 'There but for the grace of God go I.'"

The coffeemaker dinged.

"Coffee must be ready. I'll get you a cup, Ma'am."

Getting cozy with a prison guard and all that "yes, Ma'am"-ing, what was I turning into? Before I met Ms. Nelson, I assumed anyone who took a job as a guard would naturally be reactionary. If you worked in a prison, then it was because you wanted to enforce law and order. Maybe it was. Or just a way to make a living. Or a way to be tough, have a little power. It wasn't a typical female profession. It could be dangerous. Some of the guards kept their distance more than others. Seeing the same people day after day could bridge the common humanity or it could build walls. It happened on both sides. The guards had authority. Opening up required vulnerability. It took courage.

If my former comrades could see me now. That ghost would not go away. My former comrades wouldn't care what I thought, so why didn't I let go of their imaginary disapproval? Separating myself from my communist past was hard and confusing. I kept changing my mind. In the late sixties, I felt that being radical was the right thing to do, even if I was a product of being at the right place in the right time—and meeting Lee. Joining and staying with the RCP, would I have done that if not for Joe and my attachment to a small band of people championing common values? We're all products of the people around us. Would I have joined a religious cult instead? I didn't equate the RCP with a cult, but I was ready to give in and see a similarity with that and my ideology. Maybe radical zeal is necessary to keep pushing and make fundamental change. When does anything significant happen unless people take uncompromising positions? But compromise can also change things.

Being in this cerebral muddle was depressing. And what did it matter? I needed some kind of closure. Reexamining my motives and political philosophy wasn't helping. I needed to be OK with myself. I needed to let my past be.

Then there was Ms. Nelson. She was a guard. She was a good person. I respected her. She didn't fit into my previous scheme of things. I was OK with that. Maybe the analytical noise was quieting.

# Chapter 26
# Just Watch

One morning, in the hazy limbo between slumber and consciousness, I had another ghost-like visit. This time a watch appeared in my mind. It called me back to my previous punctual self. Until I shed my watch upon entering the Harris County Jail, it was a constant companion. Being on time was always important to me. I remember as a little girl asking my father what time it was and he never seemed to be badgered, looking at his watch and telling me the time as often as I asked. It confirmed my suspicion that knowing the correct time was important.

Many of my cellmates wore silver Timex watches with black elastic bands. When did it occur to me that I could get one too? Only in my dreamlike state. The watches were available for ten dollars at the commissary. They were as utilitarian as you could get, but the closest thing to a piece of jewelry we were allowed to wear.

Getting a watch became my new quest. It would make me independent. It would be a practice run for life on the outside. It was a sign of confidence. It was jewelry—not that I cared about jewelry, yet it implied some concern for my appearance in prison. It would help close the gap between my outside world and inside world, my past and future. It would keep me in the moment. There were nothing but positive vibes the more I thought about getting a watch.

In the next instant, I pictured myself checking the watch obsessively, wondering why time was moving so slowly, crawling by. My watch was another ball and chain, a constant reminder of my enslavement.

That moment of panic led to days of fretting about The Watch. It could make life worse. It would give me control. It was a small decision, but all the pros and cons battled in my mind. After my precious daytime nap was consumed with indecision, I resolved to get the damn watch.

With new purpose and pride, I put a checkmark by "watch" on my next commissary list request. I eagerly awaited its arrival. When I picked up my usual supplies, the watch was not included. A handwritten note at the bottom of the paper said that watches were not available on the weekly commissary list. I had to "drop a form" to get a watch. The fact that there was a place to check off "watch" mattered not. There was no reference on where to get a form to drop.

I was so eager to get the watch I had forgotten that nothing in prison is without rules that I was blind to. The ones you learned in orientation never seemed to apply to daily life. The only way to get the lowdown on the real workings of prison was by asking another offender. I sought out Yolanda. She told me the forms came from the assistant warden's office. I went to the assistant warden's office, and in the musky reception area there were wooden trays filled with forms. Forms for everything. Want to see the doctor? Drop a form. Need a haircut? Drop a form. How to find out where to drop the forms? Drop a form.

I found the right form, filled it out, and dropped it at the commissary manager's office. I patiently waited a few days and impatiently waited another few days. A few days turned into two weeks. There was no form to drop about getting information on a dropped form. I fumed. This wasn't something I was about to give up. I vowed to get that watch if it was the last thing I did, deep breathing more and more each day. Good air, bad air. No more gerbil spinning on a wheel in a cage going nowhere. Margret Mead was fed up observing. I made a decision to do something for myself after days of weighing the consequences. There was no way the bureaucracy was going to beat me on this one.

At last the form came back. It said that watches were currently out of stock. There was nothing about when they would be restocked. I would need to drop another form. To hell with it, I was ready to wring someone's neck.

That evening at mail call, I got a letter from Mara who was in the RCP. She wrote that she was sending a subscription of the *Revolutionary Worker* to my Gatesville address. I screamed inside. Someone else making decisions for me. Someone else controlling me. My old comrades weren't ghosts after all.

I wondered if Mara thought it was still possible to save me from bourgeoisie thinking while I was captive in prison or if sending me the *RW* was merely a knee-jerk reaction. In her letter she suggested I do something useful with my time in prison, like learn Spanish. I stormed back to my bunk, took out my legal pad, and scrawled a letter off to her, saying that she should stop the subscription to the *RW* and that I was trying to keep my sanity, not learn Spanish, and that if she thought I was a sellout, I couldn't care less.

I sealed the letter in an envelope, but was still seething. My past and present were eating me up.

I ran into the bathroom and yelled and cried with a towel over my mouth in the toilet stall. Mara, the *RW*, they uncorked a bottle of memories, second-guessing, rage. Recalling my trial, I didn't shrink away from the politics, even if I did not commit a crime. I was used as a cautionary tale of what happens when you turn against your country. While in my mind, I educated people about the difference between the government and the country, between capitalism and democracy, about a future world beyond what exists.

I didn't look out for number one, and what did I get? Prison time for someone else's crime, someone who didn't have the guts or the principles that I had. Instead of Mara, my anger zoned in on Maria. She was the traitor; she was the sellout. But what had my grand principles accomplished? And why was breaking those shackles of loyalty so daunting?

"I hate it here. I hate everybody," I yelled into the towel. I was ready to smack Connie just to see how easy it would be to get thrown in segregation. I was so sick of the rules. Sick of the roles. Being a champion of the people. Being a martyr. Being a gerbil. Being Margaret Mead. Being a failure. I hit my head on the bathroom door. Someone yelled, "Are you all right in there?" I stumbled out of the toilet and went to the sink, splashing cold water onto my face. Instead of regaining composure, my teeth started grinding. I yelled to nobody, "I'm OK," and darted back to my bunk.

I ripped a piece of paper off my legal pad and wrote to Tom about how I lied about prison and that all the woman deserved what they got and that when I got out of prison I wasn't going to give a shit about the human race, except for the kids, which was the only thing I ever did right in my life and which I screwed up too. I buried my head under my blanket and cried and cried until there was no way to cry more.

An hour later Yolanda was off her shift and she walked over to my bunk. There lay a motionless lump in the bed.

She put her hand on my back. "Are you OK?" she asked.

I didn't answer.

"What's going on?"

"Oh, Yolanda, I just feel like I can't handle this. I've tried so hard to be strong. I don't know how people can take it living here. And the stupid watch. It's like I don't exist."

"But you aren't going to be here too much longer, right? Didn't you say something about making plans for parole?"

"I guess so."

"I don't want to sound unsympathetic, but you of all people have nothing to worry about. Maybe you've been trying too hard. And by the way, I know a lot of the women are waiting on watches, the ones who have the ten dollars for a luxury."

"You're right." I blew my nose and fluffed up my hair with my fingers as Yolanda sat by my side.

"Stuff your face with biscuits, gossip about Connie, watch some stupid TV. I guarantee you'll feel better," she said.

I ripped up the letter I had written to Tom. I walked with Yolanda into the dayroom. Someone on *The*

*Young and the Restless* was having an illegal abortion. I could relate to that.

The TV, the gossip, the vision of unlimited biscuits, it required no more effort than surrender. It was comforting; it was community. It was home. No. It wasn't home.

# Chapter 27
# Why of All Places Did I
# Wind Up in Texas?

After spending two years at NYU, schooling ourselves in the revolutionary movement, Joe and I thought moving to a city on the slow end of political activity would be a better use of our talents. We joined up with likeminded cohorts and discussed where to move, concluding that a small, industrial city, Camden, New Jersey, in particular, was promising. This resulted in a field trip. Camden's smokestacks and grungy downtown, downtown being a generous term, was a turn-off. Who would leave New York City for a place like that? Nobody. We weren't sure about Camden either, but we were determined to go somewhere.

As mythic journeys often start with a sign, we came upon a book of matches from Lexington, Kentucky. The decision was made for us. Why not move to Lexington? That's all it took. We packed our newly purchased old Peugeot, and prepared to leave the East Coast. The fact that we knew nothing about Lexington, nor a soul who lived there, didn't matter.

Before leaving we attended a massive antiwar demonstration in Washington D.C., a half-million strong. From the Washington Monument to the Capitol Building, the National Mall was engulfed in an ocean of people. All these people were our people. It was one big organism. Closer in, they walked in unison, arms raised, waving banners and signs. The air was bursting with anthems and slogans. Eugene McCarthy and George McGovern spoke, and it didn't matter if they were co-opting the movement or not. Peter, Paul, and Mary, Arlo Guthrie, and Pete Seeger were singing their hearts out. The sense of history, the sense of remaking the world, it was exhilarating. I left the concert pumped and ready to "Hammer out injustice all over the land."

I was young, idealistic, and influenced by charismatic leaders. That didn't make it less real, did it? With Joe at my side, I had the courage to set sail for uncharted lands. The resolve that overtook my heart and mind came from an honest desire to help those in need. "Serve the people" was not a catchphrase, but my calling.

We left New York in the fall of 1969. I was twenty years old.

We arrived in Lexington, found a shotgun-style rental house, and unpacked all our worldly belongings, which consisted of the classics: works on revolutionary theory from Marx to Mao, and an over-abundant record collection where Bob Dylan, The Grateful Dead, Robert Johnson, Janis Joplin, Miles Davis, and Smokey Robinson resided. Joe was the music stylist and my musical tastes followed his. Fortunately he had good taste.

It was the first time Joe or I had lived in the South. Lexington is a city, but it was the country to us. One of our first days in town, a truckload of cows got loose and ran down Main Street. We were stunned, but no one else seemed surprised.

Joe and I searched for radical activity and attended a miniscule antiwar protest. I struck up a conversation with a young woman who had such a Southern twang it sounded like another language. I told her I was from New York and had just moved to Lexington.

"Oh, New York City, just come back from there," she said.

"Really?"

"Yeah. I wanted to get more into the movement and thought that sure must be the place to be. Never really fit in with these folks here. They think anyone who is antiwar or talks about civil rights is a commie. I was so happy to get away and find people who thought like me. Was I wrong! The minute I opened my mouth to talk they started laughin'. Couldn't wipe the smirks off their faces. That said it all. I was never taken seriously. They assumed I was backwards because of my accent. As if people from the South are automatically inferior. I never felt so rejected in my entire life."

"Wow, that's terrible," I said. But I knew what she meant. Growing up in New York, I had felt a certain superiority. People from the South, they had slavery, they had segregation. JFK was murdered in Dallas. MLK was murdered in Memphis. Those kind of things didn't happen up north.

"It's OK," she said. "It's better not to idolize people. There's prejudice everywhere."

I nodded my head.

Lexington was home to two colleges: The University of Kentucky, famous for its basketball team; and Transylvania University, famous for jokes about Dracula. One of the progressive professors from Transylvania took college kids on tours to Appalachia. Coal miners were in a fierce battle over union leadership of the United Mine Workers. Not exactly in college but college age, Joe and I took one of those trips.

Every small town, hamlet, and patch of land in Eastern Kentucky was visibly polarized. Signs and banners representing the different candidates for union president electrified the landscape. Some proclaimed allegiance to W.A. Boyle, who represented the old guard. More declared support for Joseph Yablonski, the reformer who spoke for the rank and file and was out to rid the union of corruption. In the otherwise sleepy "hills and hollers" of rural Kentucky, coal miners were battling to take back their union.

It wasn't only young people disgusted with the status quo. The working class was in action! All I had read about the power of the industrial proletariat was proving true in rural Kentucky. Wildcat strikes over black lung disease were gaining steam. Radicalized unions today, the revolution tomorrow. I was stirred by the coal miners' motivation and sacrifice.

At that time I didn't know what the future would hold for the mineworkers. What happened was this: On December 12, 1969, Boyle won an election widely seen as fixed. Yablonski pursued an investigation of fraud. Two weeks later Yablonski, his wife, and their daughter were murdered. Miners were incensed. The next day 20,000 mineworkers walked off the job, convinced that Boyle had orchestrated the assassinations. Years of legal proceedings persisted. Boyle was finally found guilty of masterminding the murders and was imprisoned for life.

For our last sightseeing in Appalachia, we trudged up a bumpy dirt road, jumped rocks to cross a stream, parted brambles, and came upon a small shack. A rickety lady welcomed us into her home. No electricity. No indoor plumbing. She showed us her kindergarten report card and a picture of her husband in an open coffin. I backed away from the pictures. It was a little creepy to take a picture of your deceased husband. Jews don't have open casket funerals, let alone take pictures of dead people, except for the Holocaust. The college students on the tour didn't seem to mind. As we left, the professor cupped his hands around our host and thanked her for sharing her most valuable possessions and home with us. The woman we visited held on to the professor's hands. She didn't seem to want us to leave, and I recognized how isolating rural poverty could be.

\* \* \*

In Lexington I got my first real job, at the phone company. As a teenager, I babysat. My senior year in high school, I tried to work at the new Baskin Robbins, but they didn't hire females. At that time scooping ice cream from the large tins was considered too difficult for the "weaker sex." Those were also the days when girls wore skirts to school—not as part of a uniform, but because, well, girls were supposed to look like girls. Act like girls too. In gym class we were only allowed to play half-court basketball. Even before my political awakening, these restrictions seemed silly, as I identified more with being a tomboy than a princess. After I got a cowgirl outfit for my birthday at a young age, Annie Oakley became my role model.

The phone company was an introduction to true blue-collar employment. As Lily Tomlin had done, I manually plugged long cords into a big pegboard to make a connection, answering each call with the word "operator." When the pegboard wasn't lit up with incoming calls, I learned how the operators coped with the repetition. I was taught how to flip a switch and listen in on conversations. This helped the time go by, and made we wage slaves feel like we were getting away with something, but after a while, hearing the same old conversations got tiresome.

Bluegrass music, not rock and roll, played from garage bands down my street. I borrowed Earl Scruggs and Bill Monroe albums from the Lexington Library. It didn't take long for me to sing along with the wailing high notes and fast-pickin' banjo.

Bad as I was at singing, I was good at crafts. While the men played music, the women quilted. I found my niche and learned to hand-quilt, creating a bed cover using the Viet Cong flag as a pattern for the patchwork— not that anyone in Lexington would have known what that was. Oops, my New York-stereotyping again.

Living in Lexington was an education for me and Joe, but we were not doing much in the way of educating the masses. We were lacking direction, and there were only a few radicals in town. Despite the inspiration from the coal miners, we felt cut off.

It didn't last long. Jim and Martha, a couple we knew from our NYU SDS chapter, came through Lexington on their return to Dallas, Texas, where they had grown up. They also left the East Coast to spread revolution and brought the latest news about a budding leader, Bob Avakian, who was instrumental in the Revolutionary Union (RU).

The RU formed in the Bay Area of California in 1968 and was part of SDS. From the beginning the RU was more theoretical and strategically-inclined than most radicals of the time. It boldly supported the Black Panther Party and Vietnam Veterans Against the War, and was considered a militant Maoist organization.

In 1970 four students were shot dead at protests at Kent State after Nixon sent US troops into Cambodia. Two African American students were killed at Jackson State, with many more injured at both colleges. We were ready to move on, double our ranks with Jim and Martha, and sow the seeds of revolution in Dallas.

Before leaving Lexington, Joe and I were married by a Justice of the Peace. Jim and Martha were our witnesses.

We were twenty-one years old.

Our parents back east gave us a big, post-wedding reception over the summer when we came for a visit as newlyweds. When Joe and I walked into my parents' home, we were welcomed with hugs and kisses. They were happy that at least we hadn't shunned this tradition and were interested in raising a family. My father phoned his sister, my favorite aunt, Pearl, and said, "Joe and his wife just arrived." I remember thinking, is he talking about me?

After much strife I succumbed to my mother's wishes to forgo the headband and put on a bra for our post-wedding bash. Our combined family and friends feasted on Jewish and Italian specialties. Food and family cured all that night. My father's Beefeater martinis helped too.

The next fall, Joe and I and Jim and Martha moved to the Oak Cliff section of Dallas. The four of us shared a house and worked manufacturing jobs.

We purchased secondhand furnishings for our modest, wood-frame home. The windows were plentiful and I looked forward to putting up colorful curtains to brighten up the place. Little did I suspect that this would become our foursome's first heated debate over the foundations of revolutionary principles.

Jim was outraged that I proposed putting up curtains. He said curtains were a waste of money, a perceived need cooked up by capitalist interior decorators. It was bourgeois! Once that "bourgeois" card was dealt, I was cornered. It's like pulling out a big cross in front of a vampire. You scurry for the closest dark corner available. Nobody who carries Mao's little red book wants anything whatsoever to do with the bourgeoisie.

Still I wanted curtains and knew that aesthetics was no argument. I needed to think fast.

"Um . . . working-class people have curtains . . . they don't have to be fancy. We'll fit in better."

Jim scowled.

"Curtains will give us some privacy in case of the cops," I said with authority.

That got Jim's attention. Being concerned about surveillance proved my suggestion to cover the windows was rational. It wasn't about fluff. Curtains were removed from the camp of the bourgeoisie to that of the proletariat. I won, and happily picked out fabric and sewed curtains. It made our place in Dallas homey.

In the Big D, I worked at Texas Instruments at the most tedious job of my life, testing microchips. Not only was I stuck repeating the same five-second task on a small assembly line over and over and over, but I had to raise my hand to take a bathroom break. As awful as all this was, I felt I was earning my stripes as an oppressed worker. Self-sacrifice for the cause overpowered mind-numbing labor.

We lasted a year in Dallas. Even with four of us, the revolutionary movement was not prospering. We considered it necessary to move to a city where there would be a larger concentration of industrial workers. Houston had oil field-related manufacturing and a strong longshoreman's union. It would be our next and last stop.

On our last weekend in Dallas, the city was overrun with hordes of people wearing head-to-toe burnt-orange or all red. The red T-shirts said OU. The burnt-orange T-shirts had some kind of cow symbol. Joe and I scratched our heads. Finally, we asked someone, who thought we were dumb as dirt not to know that it was Texas-OU weekend. That explained Dallas.

\* \* \*

The 1970s proceeded with chaos and contradiction. Despite the Pentagon papers, Watergate, and the massive antiwar movement, Nixon was reelected. In 1973 he started pulling U.S. troops out of Vietnam. Black Panther leaders were jailed or killed by military-style police actions. The Weathermen were in prison, or underground and alienated from whatever support they once had. The SLA (Symbolize Liberation Army) were crazies. SDS and the broad coalition of groups opposed to the Vietnam War were factionalized and fading.

What was left were a handful of organizations resolved to continue "the struggle." The RU was one of them. They developed and linked collectives nationwide. Our collective of four in Houston followed their lead. They/we/I thought that revolution was necessary and inevitable, but that premature violence, before the masses were educated and the time right, was unconstructive. They/we/I supported Mao Zedong and saw any "mistakes" he made as growing pains of a new society.

Taking this course gave me hope for the future of humankind. If I had any doubts about the truth of my position, it would unravel my entire philosophy, and where would that leave me?

One of the problems with being so convinced about anything, really, is you miss stuff. It makes for automatic blinders, not only to the possibility that one may be wrong, because that would be impossible, but to what may be going on right in front of you.

You'd think after living in Lexington and Dallas that I would have grasped the cultural challenges of moving to Houston in 1972. Nope. One of the first shockers I encountered was the Ku Klux Klan storefront in Pasadena, a blue-collar area with a backdrop of oil refinery towers. I thought the KKK was a thing of the past. To see its physical presence was disturbing and eerie. And the guns. They were sold everywhere, just an ordinary item to put in your shopping cart along with the diapers and groceries. It seems odd to think there were any fewer guns in Dallas, but I hadn't seemed to notice. It took moving to Houston for that to sink in.

In 1970 a Black Panther leader named Carl Hampton, not related to Fred Hampton, was murdered by the police on Dowling Street in Houston's third ward. Demonstrations flared at Texas Southern University, the predominantly black university in Houston. But the city itself did not experience the urban rebellions that rocked Watts, Detroit, and Chicago during those years. That the frustration level didn't manifest in Houston the same way didn't mean there wasn't outrage. Not to say that urban rebellions resolve societal problems or minimize the harm to people and communities, but they do put simmering issues in the public spotlight, without which those issues often continue to fester in the shadows.

Urban rebellions also reflect a lot about a city. Louie Welch, mayor of Houston at that time, was known for keeping a lid on dissent. And let's face it, Houston did not have a tradition of mass protests, liberal politicians, and intelligentsia. While New York City is known for its long history of European-style culture and its progressive climate, Texas is known for bibles, boots, bluebonnets, and, some would say, bigots.

*　*　*

Still Texas was not one-dimensional. It produced populists like Ann Richards, Molly Ivins, Jim Hightower, Barbara Jordan, and Mickey Leland. Austin was the site of a nationwide SDS convention in the day. In Houston there was a radical bookstore called Prairie Fire, started by homegrown leftists. KPFT, the Pacifica radio station, presented progressive news, views, and music mainly ignored by mainstream outlets. There was alternative country music. Willie Nelson recast the redneck image as a long-haired, pot-smoking, tax-evading outlaw.

We settled in Houston and I found work at the phone company again—Ma Bell, as it was called. The rest of our group worked in jobs related to the oil industry at Hughes Tool Company, Cameron Iron Works, and U.S. Steel. Jobs were plentiful and paid well. We had found our proletarian base.

As soon as I got the job at the phone company, I joined the union, the Communication Workers of America (CWA). That was one thing the old communist party and the modern day Maoists had in common, organizing in the working class. I thought the CPUSA was wrong about Mao, but I respected them for being instrumental in advocating for unemployment insurance, Social Security, and the right to organize.

In the 1970s, even in Texas, unions still were symbols of working-class strength. Shell Oil workers were striking in Houston. At Farah Pants in El Paso, four-thousand mostly Hispanic women garment workers went on strike for the right to organize a union.

I became a union job steward, spoke up at union meetings, and prodded the union leadership to take a more aggressive role with the phone company management. It was no secret that you could find CWA union stewards and Ma Bell middle management hanging out at Ernie's Ice House, swapping stories over a few too many beers.

The union leadership did not welcome my contributions. To them job stewards represented the union, which was not always in sync with the rank and file. I'm sure that some of the union members thought I was a troublemaker, while others approved of my taking a stand. Whatever it was I did as union steward, I don't remember it being particularly effective. So it was startling to be handed papers at a union meeting accusing me of "bringing the union into disrepute." How could the union call me exercising my democratic right to speak up at union meetings "bringing the union into disrepute?"

I wasn't an outsider. I paid union dues and had a good work history. When I read the indictment it stated the reason for the charge of disrepute was my communist beliefs. This was even more shocking because at the phone company I never rabble-roused about communism in any public way. At most I shared my unconventional beliefs with only a few trusted and "advanced" workers. I knew I was supposed to educate the masses about the class struggle, but it was much easier being a union militant and leaving it at that. I had no doubts about communism, but I hadn't worked for the phone company that long. I wanted to change the world, but I also wanted to be liked by my coworkers. How the CWA leadership had found out I was a communist was an enigma to me. (Much later, after securing my FBI files, I became aware of an informant in the RU at the time I was in the CWA. He, or she, monitored and reported on my activism. That could have been the missing link.)

The charges of "bringing the union into disrepute" resulted in a trial, held in a conference room at CWA headquarters on Jefferson St. in downtown Houston. Plastic tables and folding chairs were arranged in a circle. Judge, jury, prosecutor, and attorney were all union members. The prosecutor called his first witness, Irene.

"How do you know Betty Sullivan?"

She said, "Betty and I work as directory assistance operators together. One day during a split shift, I invited her over to my house, which I share with my parents. My mother and father were sitting in the living room, watching the news on TV. The Watergate scandal just broke out, and there was a special afternoon report. Betty jumped right in and talked on and on about how bad our government is. Then she tried to recruit my mother and father to communism. My parents became very upset."

I jolted in my seat. This was an outright lie. I knew this woman causally at work, but never went to her house. It was totally mind-boggling to hear someone make up this event about me that had no basis in fact.

"I didn't know what to do," Irene continued. "My grandparents came from Mexico a long time ago. We are all citizens and proud to be American. My parents were too frightened to speak up for themselves, so I told Betty to leave."

There may have been other witnesses saying they heard me talk about communism, but the only thing I firmly remember was the hurt and disbelief I felt at being portrayed as some undesirable, underhanded lout.

My union-appointed "lawyer" cross-examined the witness.

"Can you tell me the day Betty came to your house?" he asked.

Irene shifted in her chair. "I don't recall. All I remember is being very scared and upset."

I was put on the stand and allowed to tell my side of the story. I truthfully said I had never met her parents. But I have no recollection of how or if the issue of communism was dealt with at the CWA trail by the union-member lawyer defending me.

Red-baiting, a common practice of accusing radicals of being communists, whether they are or not, was something I was well aware of. The fear of communism in a country so entrenched in the capitalist system and so identified with individualism seemed unwarranted to me. If the powers that be thought their system was so great, then why worry? But this tactic of red-baiting didn't lose its appeal. If someone could be identified with a controversial group or set of ideas, then they become the other. That part of human wiring that so easily reduces individuals to groups, so easily creates stereotypes of many sorts—something we are all guilty of. Regardless of how my union lawyer dealt with the red-baiting at my little trial, it was a success.

Maybe my reputation for showing a little spunk in the face of bureaucratic leadership was appreciated by the union members' jury—they were my peers, after all, and they could identify with me—or my reaction to the accusations came off more sincerely than the prosecutor's attempts to bring *my* character into disrepute. Either way I was moved that my coworker jury was not scared off and had the courage to come to my defense. My peers found me innocent. The charges were dropped, and I was allowed to stay in the union.

* * *

A high point of moving to Houston was meeting the Iranian students at the University of Houston (UH). They organized forums and protests that brought awareness of the United States' role in supporting the Shah of Iran. The Shah ruled Iran from 1941 until 1979, and, as monarch, abolished a multiparty system of government. At that time progressive-minded people in the U.S. supported the Iranians whose movement was aimed at toppling the dictatorship. Many of the UH students returned home to join their country's revolution. The Shah was overthrown, but was replaced by the Khomeini regime, which established a Muslim state. We heard from students who stayed behind that the ones who went back to Iran were viewed as the enemy by the Khomeini forces, that they disappeared, were murdered. It was awful and incomprehensible that people I had contact with were killed for their cause.

Intellectually I knew that I shouldn't be shocked. But how could I imagine the violence of a revolution in any real way? My experience with armed revolt was abstract. These students put their lives on the line. It was overwhelming and tragic and made me both fearful and more determined.

Over the next few years, our RU collective grew to about a dozen people. Some of the members were local working class types who were attracted to the idea of equality and not afraid of the word communism. Others were former movement folks who found their way to Houston looking for jobs. They gravitated to us and our lives of purpose.

In 1975 the Revolutionary Communist Party (RCP) was founded. Most of the existing RU chapters morphed into the RCP. If you believe that capitalism is the root of inequality, and a revolution is the only way to change the balance of power, then you need a party to lead the people in overthrowing the government. Voila, the RCP.

One of my favorite slogans of the '60s was: "If you're not part of the solution, you're part of the problem." It was a catchy way to say inaction is also action. But it also summed up how I simplified problems. It was easy when the solution was defined for me by Bob Avakian. The RCP was not promoting any armed revolt ahead of time. When the crisis of inequality was at a boiling point and people were educated and willing to follow the party, only then would the RCP take power. That future gap made it comfortable for me to mash up the warm and cozy idealism of a ruler-less and ultimately democratic society that is in fact the vision of communism with the prospects of a violent revolution and the kind of repression that is inevitable when dealing with class enemies.

Yet I accepted that killing people in the name of what is necessary for the betterment of all is justified. Who doesn't proclaim their actions, however horrible, are for good? I reasoned that violence was the only way to change systems. But has real change come from war after war, people in power having their way because they know the way? Whether it is in the name of capitalism, communism, or assorted strains of fundamentalism, they all share the same idea that some things are more valuable than life itself.

# Part 4

# Chapter 28
# More Waiting

The biscuits lost their flavor. TV was a blur. Sleeping all day was easier and easier. When I was awake and mildly interactive with my peers, I grew more silent. My internal debates dried up. I didn't collect any sociological data, didn't worry about how society's injustice would be remedied. Didn't give a shit. The first of spring revival was a distant memory.

Hours went by. I didn't say a word or think a thought. Numbing self-preservation. Ironically my bunk neighbors seemed to like me more. It was as if I created a negative space, not contributing to the confusion. Commiserating with my cellmates was connection. But when they were headstrong, I couldn't compete. I buried myself in books and letters. That kept me alive.

As soon as my friends found out that they could send me books, they did. Not that it was easy. In prison, offenders are only allowed to receive books sent directly from the publisher. It required long distance phone calls, letters, and checks being sent. No one-click shopping with Amazon.

My tastes in books changed drastically in prison. I felt like I was disappointing my higher-brow friends for whom, from their perspective, which was once mine, reading went beyond enjoyment. There were standards: literary fiction, not mass-market romance or thrillers. If it was too seductive, it was a waste of time. That changed in Gatesville. When asked what books I wanted, I requested Danielle Steele instead of Virginia Woolf.

Books crossed the boundaries of life inside and outside the bars. Most everyone read something, even the women who were attached to the TV. Sharing books in this community of women, some who didn't grow up being read to, gave me hope. Plus books were the only gift we were allowed to receive from the outside world.

One day, walking back from mail call with a tightly wrapped brown package, Yolanda slowly approached me. We hadn't been hanging out quite so much since I stewed in my mute role. I slowed to a stop as Yolanda reached me and forced a grin from my face.

"What you got there?" she asked.

"Oh, you know, I'm so blessed my people send me books." I cringed inside. "Blessed" was a word I heard all the time but didn't use. I hadn't talked in so long, it felt as if I had been reincarnated as a parrot.

"Can I see?" she asked.

"Sure, let's open it together."

Yolanda and I sat up on my bunk bed, like kids embarking on a slumber party. I carefully removed the extensive tape sealing the package. As the corrugated cardboard fell away I held up a slim volume titled *Items from Our Catalog*, by Arthur Gingold. I turned a few pages and saw full-color pictures of a chloroform dog bed, edible moccasins, and a woodsy Penobscot paperclip. It was a parody of the L.L. Bean catalogue. Yolanda reached over for the book.

"What is this?"

Who in Gatesville, Texas, has ever heard of L.L. Bean or would get the idea of a parody? My head reeled. Not to underestimate my fellow offenders, it was just so out of place, so New England insider. When you live in Texas, New England is that blob in the upper right-hand corner of the U.S. map, with the names written so small you can't tell where New Hampshire starts and Vermont ends. All my fears of being foreign sprouted and steamed up like a geyser. I would have eaten the book rather than be seen reading it.

"OK, Yolanda, this is really strange. It is a book that's making fun of the L.L. Bean catalogue. Have you ever heard of that?"

"No. I've only heard of the Sears catalogue, and I don't even know whether they make those anymore," she said. "Who is L.L. Bean?"

"Good question. I hadn't thought about L.L. Bean being a real person, but that would make sense. The catalogue is from Maine. They sell lots of outdoor stuff. I'm not sure myself why making fun of that is supposed to be funny. Maybe if I was from Maine, it would make more sense."

"Well, you must have some interesting friends. At least they are trying to cheer you up."

"Now that you put it that way . . . I know it was well-intentioned. My friends have been so wonderful, but there is no denying we live in different worlds."

"That we do."

Not all books were allowed. One book banned in the Reception dorm was *Blood and Money*, a true crime murder mystery by Thomas Thompson. This was because the hit woman in the book lived in our dorm. She played a very minor part in the murder scheme, but had a major reputation among the offenders. Even though she never carried out the hit, she was implicated in a conspiracy. It was never clear to me why the book was banned. Were the authorities protecting her privacy (doubtful) or did they not want a crime sensationalized by reading about it? The fact that the book was banned magnified her role and the intrigue around it. I bought the book when I got out of prison and found only a few pages about her. Yet she was akin to a celebrity in our dorm. It was a small claim to fame for the women in my dorm to share living space with her.

Real celebrities do find their way into prison. While I was in Gatesville, David Crosby from the rock band Crosby, Stills, Nash, and sometimes Young, was incarcerated in the men's unit in Huntsville. He spent a year there on drug charges. It generated lots of excited talk in the dorm. He had his own fan club of women prison offenders.

I thought about writing David Crosby. I would tell him how much I admired his music, which was true. How I hitchhiked to Woodstock barefoot, by myself, from a campground on Martha's Vineyard, also true. We would have the vindictive Texas justice system in common, very true. A letter never materialized.

I had plenty of people to write and decided that living in my letters wasn't anything to be ashamed of. My outside reality was fuller of life than my inside reality. As spring progressed in New York, my dad wrote less about his experiences as an infantryman and more about the evolution of his garden. He finished planting sugar snap peas in one letter and put up a trellis in the next. As a kid

I never paid much attention to his gardening habit, and he didn't encourage me. It was, for him, a solitary occupation.

After our young family moved from the Bronx to Long Island, one of the first things my dad planted was apple trees. Over the years those trees towered over the yard and my parents couldn't give apples away quickly enough. Still, I didn't make the link between the semisweet Macintosh apples with my father's hand in their production. They merely appeared on our kitchen table. His letters helped me understand that digging in the soil, watering, fertilizing, and harvesting were his expressions of nurturing.

That and the cats. He kept me apprised of the new kittens that made their home in his garage. What started as feeding helpless strays became an out-of-control breeding ground. It worried me that the expanding cat colony lodging at 3 Rustic Lane was approaching crazy cat person proportions. But I lived in Texas and my brother in Brooklyn had no more influence over my dad than I did.

While my Dad's gardening life kept me anticipating his next letter, the sports section of the newspaper sustained another kind of life for me. From 1981 to 1985, during the limbo years between my conviction and going to jail, Hakeem Olajuwon and Clyde Drexler put the UH basketball team on the map. Escaping the small, flickering TV at our house, Tom, Tony, Pete, and I went to Spanky's Pizza Parlor on Telephone Road to eat supper and watch the games. Phi Slamma Jamma, the team's nickname, made it through the Sweet Sixteen, the Elite Eight, the Final Four, and on to the NCAA finals, twice. That they never won a championship was a huge disappointment, but in prison I only recalled the feeling of indulgence and joy while we rooted for the home team together.

In 1984 the Houston Rockets drafted Hakeem Olajuwon, and along with Ralph Sampson, "The Twin Towers," as they were called, led the Rockets to win after win down the stretch towards the NBA championship during that Gatesville spring. I soaked up every statistic pertaining to basketball, one-on-one with my family, linking my fate with the Rockets. We were both heading into the finals and every win of theirs was a win for me.

Houston was Clutch City, and I clutched those positive vibes. I embodied that resilience when I wrote to my friends. I wanted them to think of Betty Sullivan as worthy of their support. Not weak. The truth was every miserable day dragged on and dragged me down. Maybe because I was waiting for parole and the end being near made time slower. Maybe I was getting disenchanted with my cellmates. It was harder and harder to shine a positive light on my dreary life. My plummeting spirit was channeled through daily letters to Tom. The more life in prison weighed on me, the more I felt possessive of Tom.

Tom's letters back to me were reassuring, but they stirred up conflicting emotions. He had the kids, coworkers, friends, warm bodies to wrap himself around. He was getting so much sympathy and kudos for being the model stepdad. He was a hero. Even if some of our friends speculated that his freedom was at my expense.

How could I be jealous? He was mentally and physically there for the kids. I just had to exist and let time take its toll. Where was all that oppressed-worker will power I once had that helped me endure anything?

I was even jealous of how Tom was so much more eloquent than me. He could express my feelings better than I could. Damn English major. When I read his letters, we were in unison and apart.

*Love,*
*Tursday afternoon, I feel so weird. Shaky, tentative, blocked, unconfident, not quite despairing. Moving very slowly. Irritable, not wanting to be bothered. Needy, wanting to be comforted.*
*I'm getting tired of this whole thing. Weary is probably the word, yes. Oh, we are getting stronger, we are being forced back into our deeper reserves. It is harder now. That momentum is slowed, and it's like almost a sag is happening. A droop in time. Like the blues: where it's so pervasive you can't conceptualize it anymore. You are just there. Knee-deep in shit. I've been feeling resentful as hell, bordering on self-pity. Sunday was hard.*
*I went with the kids to Ingrando Park, with bicycles and baseball gloves to play catch, but it was boring. We all felt awful and lonely. Seeing all the families, couples, and people hanging out and feeling good. I missed you so sorely. And felt resentment. Not just hatred of the system, but of Texas too. What kind of place is it where women are so fucking backward that they hang a strong one of their own? They have renounced their human being-ness and cannot be dealt with as such.*
*When I was sitting Saturday I started crying, thinking about Tony and how much love he needs. Don't worry, the kids are doing fine. But I know how much they are hurting inside even if they don't always show it. I think all the time about leaving this place*

*and going somewhere and starting anew, and I feel no qualms about "taking the kids away from their father." We'll talk about it. In my current state nothing is rational . . .*

His bitterness, how I sympathized. I didn't let myself feel bitter towards him. I needed him too much. I tried to build myself up thinking that he needed me too. That I wasn't replaceable, that I still made him think and feel. I was the other side of him, and he was the other side of me. He was in his own prison. I would try to understand our individual paths, our like-mindedness and our differences. He was a saint to the kids. That was the most important thing. Buddhism was saving him, it must be good. If it wasn't my path, that was OK. If we could endure this, we could endure anything. Yet the fear that something would drag him away from me persisted. I clutched harder.

# Chapter 29
# The Story of Joe Torres
# and Moody Park

Chicano activists in the 1960s raised awareness of Cinco de Mayo as a day to honor Mexican heritage and pride. In states with large Hispanic populations, the day is filled with parades, mariachis, and Mexican folk dancing, the night with cerveza and margaritas.

All across Houston, in bars, cantinas, and ice houses, revelers celebrated Cinco de Mayo through the sweaty night on May 5, 1977. A young Mexican American Vietnam veteran named Joe Campos Torres was among them, in one such place on the East End. With the alcohol flowing freely, a few of the men exchanged words and a scuffle broke out. Several police officers arrived on the scene and Joe Torres was handcuffed and put under arrest for public intoxication and disorderly conduct. He did not go peacefully. By the time they brought him to jail, he was so badly beaten, the admitting officer refused to book him, and told the arresting officers, "Take him to Ben Taub hospital, we can't have anyone looking like that in here."

The cops pushed Torres back into their car and sped off. Instead of going to the hospital, he was taken to Buffalo Bayou, to an area known as "the hole." He was thrown in the water, left to drown. By some accounts he was still handcuffed, and the police reportedly said,

"Let's see if the wetback can swim." Joe Torres's body was washed up at the McKee Street Bridge near downtown Houston the next day.

When word of the death of Joe Torres leaked, a shockwave of public outrage hit Houston like a tsunami. Hispanic and liberal/progressive groups quickly organized protests that gave voice to the anger of the community. Within days a broad coalition of organizations and individuals formed, exposing an array of problems in the police department. Members of the RCP sprang into action and initiated "People United to Fight Police Brutality." The rallying cry, "Justice for Joe Torres," was heard from the University of Houston, through the second, third, and fifth wards, to downtown City Hall.

Whenever communists get involved in mass movements, they often get a lot of heat from all sides. People in power are quick to use the presence of communists to discredit a movement. "It's the communists stirring up trouble again, don't listen to them." Other activists often grumble about communists. They accuse them of participating in a movement only to promote themselves and their brand of revolution. Some may care less about ideology, but fear reds will alienate other participants. All valid objections. I'm sure there were times when members of the RCP pissed people off, pushing the *RW* newspaper, ranting about revolution like a broken record. Despite that behavior I believe that "People United to Fight Police Brutality," or "People United" as it came to be known, contributed much more than it detracted from the struggle for justice for Joe Torres.

My personal involvement got off to a slow start. Pete was born on May 17, twelve days after Joe Torres was killed. It was a little odd having a newborn just when this huge political struggle was taking off. The blessed event was hardly the center of attention. It didn't stop me from being overtaken with a surge of love. Our new little baby was perfect. Having two children was something I always wanted. It made me think about women refugees, how they had to just keep going, nature having its own timetable.

Tony was two-and-a-half and immediately took to his new little brother. Joe was a proud poppa again, despite being as busy as ever in all things RCP.

My mother came down from New York to help out as she had done when Tony was born. This time she found herself in the midst of manic activity. Banners being made, flyers produced, the phone rang constantly, people were in and out of the house, political strategy being forged day and night. My mom shrugged it off and was an immense help. Or maybe it would be more apropos to say she dug in and provided a sanctuary for me and my newborn. Amid the chaos she prepared bagels and lox, brought as a treat from New York as you couldn't get it in Houston at the time. She washed dishes, did laundry, and swept the floor between meetings while I napped. She cooked meals and made sure Tony was getting attention, too. I would have been a zombie if she hadn't been around. I hope she realized how much it meant that her concerns about my political activity dissolved when it came to helping me and bonding with her new grandson.

\* \* \*

The murder of Joe Torres and subsequent events brought out a new level of harassment against political activists. Members of "People United" were regularly photographed at demonstrations and followed home by unmarked police cars. There were numerous arrests. Carrying "Justice for Joe Torres" signs and chanting "The People United Will Never Be Defeated" made you a target.

My idea of peaceful demonstrating didn't include being intimidated by the cops. I admit to a certain bravado that was not always smart. But I wasn't out to break any laws. Being militant was not the same as being violent.

Throughout 1977 marches, protests, and all the organizing to pull that together continued. The murder of Joe Torres followed the exposure of the "throw-down gun" tactic by Houston Police. A seventeen-year-old, white teenager, Randall Webster, was chased down and killed by a policeman. A gun was found at the scene, inferring Randall Webster's murder was justified. It was revealed that the gun had been planted at the scene by the cops. Bobby Joe Connors was killed by police while he reached in his back pocket and pulled out a bible. Tales of the KKK recruiting in the police locker room spread. This exposure had many Houstonians questioning the police, from their policies to what role they played in minority communities. Eventually charges were filed against the officers responsible for Joe Torres's murder. People United kept the issue alive in the public eye as many people looked to the courts for justice that would make things right.

In May of 1978, the next year, two of the policemen were tried on state murder charges in Huntsville, Texas—

of all places to get a fair trial, where the city is defined by the prison system. The all-white jury convicted the police officers of misdemeanor criminal negligent homicide. They received probation and a one-dollar fine.

The verdict coincided with the one-year anniversary of Joe Torres's death. This weighed heavily on the minds of the predominately Hispanic community who were in Moody Park to celebrate Cinco de Mayo. Members of People United went to the park early in the day, passing out flyers condemning the verdict. Afterward they left to picnic at a home nearby. They gathered together, munching tacos, before focusing on the next phase of political organizing.

The afternoon get-together was relaxed until Arturo, a teenager who hung around People United, bounded over from the park, breathing hard. He excitedly told the gathering, "Some guys at the park started acting rowdy." Then out of nowhere the police moved in for a bust. People got up from their lawn chairs and blankets and went running over, shouting and waving their fists, telling the cops to get the hell away. More cops came, and more people acted crazy. Then the cops got scared and backed away. Everyone at the park started cheering and yelling, "Justice for Joe Torres."

Upon hearing this news, the three members of the RCP most active in People United, Tom, Mara, and Travis, returned to Moody Park with a bullhorn and banner, cheering the crowd on for standing their ground against the police. The tables had turned. The mood was celebratory; it was a liberation moment.

More and more people from the park took the party into the streets. The sun started going down and the effects of drinking going up. No one knows who threw the first rock that crashed into a store window or who lifted the first TV. While the opportunistic looting intensified, the police reassembled in the north part of the park and marched back down Fulton Street in unison. A line of batons and shields confronted the crowd. Instead of "Viva Joe Torres," Travis used the bullhorn to calm the crowd. It was too late. Tom, Maria, and Travis soon left, as they had no way to stop the escalating violence.

Buildings and police cars went up in flames, row upon row of store windows were smashed, broken into, and vandalized. One reporter got stabbed and another run down. Approximately forty people were arrested before the police regained control.

Later that week police rounded up Tom, Mara, and Travis, and booked them with misdemeanor and felony riot charges. All were promptly put in solitary cells in the county jail. Their bond was set at half-a-million dollars. The message: Outside agitators started the riot. The passive residents near Moody Park would never think to raise a hand against the system or act against their oppression.

Whether you think what happened in Moody Park was senseless violence or righteous rebellion or some of each, holding the RCP responsible was using them as a scapegoat.

A year later, at the trial of the Moody Park Three, as Tom, Mara, and Travis were called, a man who had been in the cell next to Tom testified in court. He said that Tom bared his soul to him and admitted that he brought a pickup truck to Moody Park, filled with beer and baseball bats, to incite a riot. This was fabricated as well as ludicrous. How easy for law enforcement to put words into someone's mouth. One of the jurors in the case described the testimony of government witnesses like this: "Some of them just told blatant lies."

Travis and Mara were convicted of felony riot and sentenced to five years' probation. Tom received probation for slightly lesser charges. Their convictions were overturned in 1984 as the appeal courts asserted that the riot statute was too broad. It allowed that everything that happened at a riot could be pinned on anyone who was there. In 1985 they pled no contest to misdemeanor riot without serving any prison time. Tom was quoted as saying, "I don't believe the cops who killed Joe Torres were prosecuted with the same vigor that we were."

The Justice for Joe Torres struggle and Moody Park events were catalysts. They threw long-standing problems between the police and the Hispanic community into view. Three officers connected with the Joe Torres murder were later convicted of federal civil rights violations and served nine months in prison. The Houston Police department established an internal affairs division and hired more minority police. A group of Spanish-speaking officers was formed at HPD. The days of police chief Pappy Bonds flaunting Houston's redneck image were no longer acceptable.

These reforms were meager compared to fundamentally altering the system, and were not part of the communist playbook. It is clear that the issue of police brutality, its relationship to inequality, and what to do about it, has not gone away. How or whether real change can happen under our current system is way beyond me.

The power of people's resistance, the change that occurs when people act together, changes the people that act together. That was the most meaningful change of all.

When I got arrested in 1981 the Joe Torres/ Moody Park movement had long subsided, yet the Criminal Investigation Division of the Houston Police kept the RCP on their radar. The RCP nationwide was being closely watched by the FBI. Thinking about this in Gatesville made me wonder if putting a communist in prison was payback. I wasn't thinking conspiracy, but grudge. I was married to Tom, one of the notorious Moody Park Three. How would the police know that my allegiance to the RCP had waned, or would they care? I still showed up at the occasional protest. I was the weak link in the herd. I was a thorn in somebody's side. People get screwed all the time for how they appear, not what they've done.

# Chapter 30
# Parlez Vous Francais?

The word *parole* has French origins. It means *word* or *honor*, as in keeping your word. The idea is that parolees are granted their freedom on "their honor" to conduct themselves in a law-abiding manner. Honor is further kept in check with a minimum of monthly visits to an assigned parole officer. Parole officers also supervise probationers, which has the effect of confusing the two terms. The primary difference is that probation is an alternative to incarceration and parole occurs after incarceration. Parole allows offenders to serve the remaining portion of their sentences supervised in the community.

To be eligible for parole, I needed to make a "plan." I heard the women in my dorm talking about making a plan for parole, but thought it was merely chat about what they would do when they left prison. I hadn't realized that it was a required part of the parole process.

The core part of the plan was coming up with a confirmable place to live and having a job lined up prior to release. The rest was character letters. For me having a home and family to return to was a given. The management at Texas Art Supply did not hesitate to put in writing that I had a job waiting for me. I wondered how many other offenders had an acceptable place to live, let alone an employer willing to back a con.

Tom sent me copies of the letters from my old boss as well as letters from what seemed like everyone I knew, attesting to my good character and value as a community member. They said I was not a threat to society and did not belong in jail. They assured the authorities that I had a job, friends, and family supporting me. So many letters referred to me as a good mother and that keeping me away from my children was hurting both them and me. Getting praised as a parent was the highest compliment I could imagine.

Reading those letters felt like reading my own eulogy. In the process it felt like part of me had died—that part that saw class struggle as the ultimate definer of relationships. The RCP was no longer the core of my existence, even if it was still part of me. My relationship to my past was not going to be something I could shut in a coffin. My quest for truth was as much personal as it was intellectual. It was OK to focus on my family, my friends, my release. It wasn't just OK; it was what mattered.

I thought about my dad and how I had never felt closer to him. He sent a letter in my support, proudly proclaiming that he was an infantryman in World War II and was one-hundred-percent behind his daughter. It started me on a crying spell.

When my father started writing to me in jail, he signed his letters with the single letter "P." Then he signed off with "Phil." "Phil" progressed to "Love, Phil." Then "Love, ~~Phil~~ Dad." By the time I got to prison, it was all "Love, Dad." I had hunkered down with him in the foxholes of France, and he held my chaffed hands while washing dishes in the prison kitchen. The letters he sent to me were good for him, too. This was the only time he ever shared his war experiences.

After my mother died, my father and I grew closer. Tony and Pete were the only grandkids and they spent significant time in the summer with my dad. But even as I drifted away from the RCP, we avoided talking about politics. I hadn't told my father I was arrested for spray painting, nor that I was going to jail. I didn't want him to be disappointed in me or worry. Plus I never believed it would amount to anything. Once I got the news I would be incarcerated, it seemed too late. With my father on the East Coast, I thought I could avoid the uncomfortable revelation... "By the way, Dad, did I ever mention anything about a felony to you?" Distance was protection. When my mother was dying of cancer, my dad did not reveal the extent of her illness. Keeping bad things inside, not wanting to make the ones you care about worry, keeping yourself protected, too, and separated—I had repeated the pattern when it came to my father. It was Kelly who told my dad I was going to jail. Another unbelievably insightful act by a friend who knew we needed each other.

With my letters of recommendation in place, there was one final thing needed for my parole packet. The sheriff, district attorney, and judge who had handled my case would be informed and could voice a protest or an approval, or not respond. This required a trail of paperwork from Gatesville to Austin to Houston. I was mildly worried about my nemesis Judge Walker being a problem. But I didn't get worked up about it. After my meltdown from the watch, and the Mara letter, even anxiety was too exhausting. Time would pass. It was out of my hands. Everything was in place for my parole plan. There was nothing to do but wait. Wait. I was getting good at something in prison.

# Chapter 31
## Wendy Saves the Day

What rescued me from the quicksand-pull of anger, resentment, and increasing, self-isolating moodiness were two things: Wendy Riss's front-page article about my case, which came out in the March issue of *Houston Style* magazine, and the Justice for Betty Sullivan benefit at Diverse Works.

When Jack took up my cause, he met Wendy, a young journalist recently relocated to Houston. She listened to Jack's pleas about the injustice of my case and they both charged off to dig deeper into the details. The first order of business was to verify that I wasn't the spray painter. They spoke to Tom, and he revealed his involvement with Maria. I think that was the first time Tom felt able to be truthful, and he was tremendously relieved to be done with hiding any longer. Jack and Kelly wanted to track down Maria. Tom had no information about her whereabouts. She could be anywhere. Jack and Kelly tried to connect with the RCP for more information, but that was a dead end.

Jack and Wendy went on to do their own investigative work about the undercover world of the criminal investigation department of the Houston police. Wendy interviewed Sam Nuchia, head of the CID, who stated that the CID's three basic functions were to "keep track of organized crime, gather information about potential terrorists, and to work with the Secret Service for the protection of foreign and national dignitaries." How that translates to spying on local activists was not addressed, unless participating in democracy beyond the ballot box makes you a potential terrorist.

In the article, Wendy highlighted an ACLU lawsuit from the mid 1970s challenging the police's surveillance of thousands of Houstonians who weren't involved in any sort of criminal activity or civil disorder but participated in progressive movements. Wendy also interviewed Gertrude Barnstone, a longtime Houston artist and veteran liberal activist who was part of the lawsuit. Barnstone said the CID was a regular presence at Free South Africa, anti-nuclear rallies and demonstrations, and ACLU meetings.

Wendy tracked down Judge George Walker. Per *Houston Style*, he asserted that the case was tried like any other case and insisted that the trial was fair and impartial. Yet he said he would not be surprised to learn the members of the jury felt I deserved to go to jail because of the content of the message rather than the graffiti itself.

Laura Ann Finley, a member of the jury that Wendy interviewed, said "that the contents of the message were very upsetting and people like that shouldn't be allowed to just get away with it." When asked whether she agreed that, had the message been "God Bless America," the verdict would have been the same, she answered, "I don't think . . . No, it wasn't the fact that she spray-painted on a building but what it actually said."

When I heard that the article was published and my picture was on the front page of *Houston Style* magazine, I felt publicly vindicated. It validated all the work of Jack, Kelly, and Beth, the work they poured into the Justice for Betty Sullivan committee. When Wendy visited me in jail and prison, it instilled my spirit with dignity. Using my guilty verdict and incarceration to make a political point kept me whole. This was my platform. This was where I knew myself. Despite the inner turmoil about what seemed like everything, the Betty Sullivan who got sentenced to two years for spray painting that she didn't do had worth.

About the same time that the article came out, Jack, Kelly, and Beth organized a benefit for me at Diverse Works, where Beth had a studio. That was the other thing that made a difference. Several area artists donated their work for sale, raising funds for lawyers who were preparing an appeal to the Supreme Court. One local artist donated his time and talent to create a hand-silkscreened T-shirt for the event. The image on the front was of an arm raised high. Instead of a clenched fist, the fingers clutched a spray paint can. Mel Chin, whose metal palm tree sculpture marked the entrance to the Houston Contemporary Art Museum, donated a piece for auction. I was floored that an artist of such recognition found my plight worthy.

Wendy's article and the benefit reminded me of what Kelly did on her own months earlier at the Lawndale Art and Performance Center, where the University of Houston's Women and Peace conference was held in January, 1986. On opening night they had a Peace Fence and women contributed images of doves that were affixed to the railing. Kelly wrote me about this and I sent her a simple pen-drawn dove to contribute to the peace fence a few weeks before I was transferred to Gatesville. Kelly hung up my peace dove along with a copy of the *Houston Post* article entitled "Mother of 2 Facing Prison for Mischief." She included her own explanation about my circumstances. It read, in part: "Those of you with an interest in feminism and its relationship to world peace should feel a kinship with Betty Sullivan. If one person is treated unjustly for their beliefs, it is a great danger for us all."

How many people became sympathetic to my case because of my friends' efforts I never knew, but I received more mail—from Gertrude Barnstone, from the director of the Houston Area Women's Center, from people I didn't know. One woman said she had a daughter my age who was active in the peace movement, and she could see her daughter being in my shoes. She praised me for being brave and contributed money to my legal fund. She hoped to hasten my release. It was incredibly touching to read her words and feel a mother's concern extended to me. Knowing my friends were making such an effort to bring awareness to my case was humbling and exciting and had me thinking of myself as a political prisoner, which seemed more than I deserved.

When I thought about political prisoners, they were people like Nelson Mandela, who spent a lifetime in prison. During the 1960s and 1970s, freeing Angela Davis, Leonard Peltier, and countless others was intrinsic to the freedom struggles going on. How many people all over the world are imprisoned for political beliefs, I wondered. I wasn't so unique after all. As for my cellmates, depending on how you weighed in, many of them could be considered political prisoners too.

The celebrity political prisoners didn't draw attention to themselves, but to what they believed in, what they were punished for. The treatment of dissenters generated deliberation. I still craved that discourse. But what had I done? My friends were the ones who deserved the credit. They thought it was important enough to take a stand and make my situation public.

There was no one inside whom I felt comfortable sharing this information with, not even Yolanda. I did not want to draw attention to myself, even if she would be happy for me, and her status, once she was close to a mini celebrity, would increase.

My friends responded to my defense with the same speed and tenacity five months after I was incarcerated as they did my first day in jail. I felt more like a victim of circumstance than a political prisoner. Yet my friends wrote of my inspiration and character. Maybe it was the Margaret Meade-like reporting on the prison experience that made me look commendable. The need to inform the outside about what life was like on the inside was as much an anesthetic to my daily pain as my mission.

Even if I was in prison, even if I was out of the RCP, even if I couldn't make up my mind whether I had spent most of my adult life as an intolerant ideologue or a devoted freedom fighter, being "political" still had its attraction. But I needed to put it in perspective. Life with a purpose didn't have to mean one purpose. Life could be embraced and respected, not confined by a platform of judgments. What had fired up my friends to act boldly on my behalf was not some abstract principle, but empathy.

My creative, driven friends: their feelings of connection to me, their witness to my suffering, their sense of injustice, crossed boundaries that my intellectual thinking only skimmed. They seemed so much more whole than me. So much less conflicted. Their passions were not hierarchical and graded. Passion for the masses number one, passion for individuals number two. I underestimated how dangerous intellectual passion could be. I thought the euphoria I felt in fighting the system was proof that I was a good person and truly cared about people. Since I was good, and communism was based on a science, it was a faultless embrace. I didn't realize that passion locked me into looking at individuals, people, society, and economics in a closed, one-sided way. Everyone, except for those drawn to Marxism, was wrong. Only people like me saw the world the way it truly is. Self -justification found a way to repress any contradiction that challenged my worldview. *They* saw crimes and *we* saw mistakes. I had an answer for everything. I had the right solution before the question was asked. And it felt good. But it wasn't good.

# Chapter 32
# War

April 15, 1986, two guards came into the sleeping area of our dorm in the middle of the day and said, "Ya'll come out to the dayroom."

*Now what?* I thought as I hopped off my bunk to join the others putting down their crochet hooks and pens, filing into the already crowded dayroom. The guard turned the TV channel to NBC news. There was President Reagan projecting serious, confident eye contact with the TV cameras.

"My fellow Americans . . . the United States launched a series of strikes against the headquarters, terrorist facilities, and military assets that support Mu'ammar Qaddafi's subversive activities. The attacks were concentrated and carefully targeted to minimize casualties among the Libyan people with whom we have no quarrel." (Smile). "From initial reports, our forces have succeeded in their mission . . . I warned Colonel Qaddafi we would hold his regime accountable for any new terrorist attacks launched against American citizens . . . On April 5th in West Berlin, a terrorist bomb exploded in a nightclub frequented by American servicemen . . . This monstrous brutality is but the latest act in Colonel Qaddafi's reign of terror. The evidence is now conclusive that the terrorist bombing of La Belle discotheque was planned and executed under the direct orders of the

Libyan regime . . . We have solid evidence about other attacks Qaddafi has planned against the United States installations and diplomats and even American tourists . . . Today we have done what we had to do. If necessary, we shall do it again. . .

"For us to ignore by inaction the slaughter of American civilians and American soldiers, whether in nightclubs or airline terminals, is simply not in the American tradition. When our citizens are abused or attacked anywhere in the world on the direct orders of a hostile regime, we will respond so long as I'm in this Oval Office. Self-defense is not only our right, it is our duty . . . He counted on America to be passive. He counted wrong. I warned that there should be no place on Earth where terrorists can rest and train and practice their deadly skills. I meant it. I said that we would act with others, if possible, and alone if necessary to ensure that terrorists have no sanctuary anywhere. Tonight, we have.

"Thank you, and God bless you."

"This is the end of days," someone howled. "This is the beginning of World War III," another voice screeched. Everyone was grabbing the person seated closest to them and hugging tightly. The whimpering and tears were contagious, like some virus of fear spreading from person to person. Even the women who were incarcerated for years looked bewildered. It was scary hearing this news in this isolated colony.

With the broadcast of attacks in Libya, it sounded like a real war was possible. Hearing anything traumatic when you are far from family makes you feel farther. The gulf between Gatesville and our various homes across Texas was growing with the hysteria. Yet the reports from the outside world meant something to us, and in that way we were part of that world more than ever.

All through the night, the drum of planes taking off and landing from neighboring Fort Hood defined my sleep. A prison close to a military base, this must be the belly button of the belly of the beast.

The next morning the TV was turned on at dawn, which was never the case. The talking heads' speculation created more fear. I was getting swept up in the frenzy. Best thing to do was wait and read the newspaper—not that I expected it to be objective, just less panic driven.

First in line at mail call that day, I ravaged the paper for news. The paper reported that the US launched two hundred US aircraft and dropped sixty tons of bombs on Qaddafi's military headquarters. Qaddafi escaped. One of his baby daughters was killed and two of his young sons were injured. All tolled thirty-seven people died, including some civilians. What would happen now? The thought that World War III would take place while I was stuck in prison seemed like too much irony. It started being funny and ridiculous. I wondered if irony and denial were my coping mechanism.

Yolanda came over to my bunk the minute she got off work the next day.

"I don't know what to think. My first reaction was, *Go, America, we can't back down.* Now I'm worried where this will all end," she said.

"I know what you mean. I don't know if a big country like ours going after a small one like Libya will have other countries taking sides."

Jenny heard us talking and popped up her head. "I say fight fire with fire."

More women gathered around our bunks.

"The Libyans deserve it."

"More war won't help anyone."

"It's not so smart to trust everything you hear."

"I don't know whether bombing is going to create more enemies than friends."

"I don't want to let those terrorists get away with anything."

"I wonder what would become to us if there was some kind of world war."

"Maybe they'd let us out of prison!"

"Yeah, that would be something."

"I say bomb the hell out of them and let's get out of here."

"Where the Hell is Libya anyway?"

Yolanda piped up. "I heard on the news that Libya is in Africa. Had no idea. But it's more Arab than African. And they have a lot of oil."

"Oil, so that's what it's all about."

\* \* \*

For the next seventy-two hours, our routine was punctuated by politics. We debated whether the Libyans deserved the bombing or not, whether it was all about oil, whether violence begets violence, whether it was all meant to be.

In the following days, a pro-Libyan Palestinian group killed two Americans and one British hostage. Then somehow it all mysteriously blew over the same way it blew in.

Our world affairs salon was not deeply intellectual, it didn't influence international events; despite that, it was energizing. The minutia of everyday life was not the only thing on our minds. Sharing ideas sparked something in me and the women I lived with. We all had something, some comment, off the wall or not, to say about the world beyond the prison bars.

Wrangling over political ideas, fear, far-out fantasies, all were up for grabs. For a short while I was in my element, without feeling obliged to promote anything. My opinions were still on the distrust-the-government side, but I didn't support terrorism and didn't have to worry about not sounding revolutionary enough—or not having an answer, as much as I missed having an answer.

Although "all meant to be" was something most everybody but me agreed on, discussing our different opinions about the conflict with Libya was empowering. We shared a desire to understand what was happening in the world. That was connected to our concern for what would happen to our families if there was war. The inside and outside world meshed. What we talked about mattered. It made us feel like we mattered. It was bonding second only to Farrah Fawcett and *The Burning Bed*.

# Chapter 33
# Release

One early morning, on my way back to the main cell from the kitchen, I was intercepted by a guard. She told me the assistant warden wanted to see me. This only happens if you get in trouble or to learn your release date.

The guard escorted me to a small reception area in the administration building. She left me standing there, and said, "The assistant warden will come out of her office and see you soon."

There were no chairs, only a plastic folding table stacked with forms. The assistant warden opened her door, called me into her office, and told me to sit down. Fortunately she wasn't going to stand and talk to me; my legs were shaking as I wondered about my fate.

As she sat down and rummaged through papers on her desk, I looked at the wall behind her. There hung commemorative plaques and a black and white picture of Gatesville when it was a boys' home. One of my cellmates said that the assistant warden believed that Gatesville was in fact haunted by ghosts. That anyone would want to work in a haunted prison seemed strange. The convicts are kindred spirits, but an administrator might want to watch her back.

I had no idea what time it was, watch-less still, but the wait seemed to be endless while I sat knocking my knees together in my chair. The phone rang, the assistant warden answered it and blurted out, "Call me in another minute," and hung up.

*Why can't the bitch find my papers?* I thought to myself, feeling proudly like a hardened criminal.

She looked up as if she heard my thoughts. Barely moving her lips, and sounding like a recording, she said, "Ms. Sullivan, your release date is set for Wednesday, April 30. Your family will receive written notification. Prison transportation will drop you off at the bus station and you will receive a voucher for bus fare anywhere in the state, taken out of your inmate trust fund or earnings. You are allowed one collect phone call on the Sunday before your release. Do you have any questions?"

Release date equaled going home. It only began to register.

"No questions and thank you."

"I'll get a guard to get you back to your dorm."

I remained stuck to my chair.

"You can get up now and wait in the reception area," she said.

I got up and drifted out of the office. "Ms. Sullivan," I hadn't heard that since my trial. When I married Tom, I went back to my maiden name of Baer. But it was Betty Sullivan who went to prison, and once incarcerated, inmates never had a last name. I flinched at being called Betty Baer growing up. It sounded like Donald Duck's sister. Upon my release it would change back to Baer, and it wouldn't change again no matter what. Having Donald Duck as a brother wasn't so bad. I could have been Ginny Gerbil if I had thought about it.

After I got back to my dorm, the only thing on my mind was going to pee. Grabbing my toilet paper from the lock box as I ran to the bathroom, I imagined how wonderful it would be to have toilet paper next to the toilet.

I returned to my bunk and seized all my belongings and dumped them on my bed. Letters and crochet items to take home stacked here; pens, pencils and extra writing supplies to give away to special people. Toiletries for the B-list. It was silly. I wasn't going anywhere for several days, and why tempt fate? I shuffled everything back together and stuffed it away.

I grabbed my pen and paper, but my hand started shaking. I couldn't hold the pen steady enough to write. I was so eager to complete The Last Letter that I would ever compose behind bars. My mind calculated how long the mail delivery would take. When was the final day I could send a letter without it arriving at its destination after I was released? How wonderful to simply write a letter and let it fly away without viewing it as some carrier pigeon finding its way home.

I set out to locate Yolanda. She was still at work. Jenny was napping. Excitement was growing in me, and it felt like I was pregnant and didn't want to blurt out the news to just anybody, yet had no idea how much longer I could hold it in. I thought about the one phone call. It would have to be to my dad.

I had the same worries most ex-cons have about what to do next. Working at Texas Art would be a temporary solution. The limbo was over. The previous jobs I had held, working for the phone company and the Post Office, a stint in Dallas at Texas Instruments, were chosen because they were places to organize. Thinking about work that was meaningful to me and not part of a master plan was something that I hadn't considered since high school. At that time I had heard about a little-known profession called occupational therapy. In the sixties OTs were often portrayed as basket weavers. Occupational therapy appealed to my crafty side. But the underlying message was using your hands to heal your mind. I hadn't thought about that in twenty years. I wondered if all the crocheting experience from prison would offset the felony conviction.

Yolanda crept up on me and approached my bunk with a big smile on her face.

"This is my last week. Can you believe it? I'm going home."

"I knew it."

"I'm not going to even ask you how you know what you know. I've stopped trying to figure things out."

"No, you haven't." Yolanda laughed.

"OK, psychic, you have first dibs on all my goods. But I don't think any of my chocolate stash will be left."

"Thanks. I'm just so happy for you. Really. People like you make this place bearable."

"That's what I was thinking about you."

As word filtered around the dorm that I had a release date, the ritual of saying goodbye ensued. Jenny hugged me and asked if she could have any extra coloring implements that were left over. Connie came up to me, wished me well, and asked me to drink a margarita for her. I would be happy to oblige. If anyone successfully made jailhouse hooch, she would know. Saying goodbye brought out the best in everyone, and if anyone was jealous, she didn't show it, at least not to me. It was a celebration when anyone got sprung from the joint.

On my last Sunday in prison, I was led to the administration building where the pay phone was. I was given a quarter to put in the slot, which bounced back in the coin return after announcing my collect call to Phil Baer.

"Dad, how are you?

"Everything is fine here."

"I got my release day, I'm going home April 30th."

"Yes, I know, Tom called to tell me."

"Oh."

"I'll talk to you when you get home."

"OK, Dad."

I wanted to tell him how the daily words he wrote had gotten me through the most hellish times in prison. I wanted to say, "I love you." I wanted to hear "I love you" back. I hung up the receiver feeling cheated. I knew my dad was not one for long phone conversations, but this was my one phone call from prison. It was like talking to the old Dad. I worried what might happen to the loving connection we built through letter writing.

The night before my release, I was issued civilian clothes to wear out the prison gates into the free world—navy, stretched-out stretch pants and a wrinkled, brown, button-down, long-sleeved shirt, the ugliest things, and never mind that they didn't match. But I didn't care about clothes, right?

That night I rocked and rolled in bed and barely slept. For once it didn't matter. I got up early and took my final shower. The water falling on my body relaxed my tense muscles. The sounds around me, toilets flushing, pipes groaning, the scent of shampoo, all had become a familiar background gone unnoticed. The women here will go on. Life has an agency of its own.

I got dressed in the Salvation Army seconds. It was strange to be out of my whites. There was something about a uniform. That comforting lack of decision-making and individuality appealed to me. Whatever it meant to pay more attention to my appearance still seemed like more trouble than it was worth. But I felt disgusting in the outfit I put on on my final day in prison. I wanted to look like a normal person when I set foot into the real world, not prison property. I was ready to take back my life.

One of my cellmates told me to write to my husband to bring a set of my own clothes to change into as soon as I could, after I was deposited at the Greyhound station following my release. Even though it seemed trivial at the time, I wrote to Tom and asked him to take along a pair of my jeans and sandals when he came to pick me up. It was one of the best pieces of advice I got.

With my bags packed with letters and craft creations, I said my final goodbyes, glad that my arms were not free to hug anyone. Not because I wouldn't miss some of them, but my focus was the future, not the past. My offender identity was peeling away as the minutes towards my exit grew closer.

I signed my release papers, stuffed the multiple copies in my pocket and filed on the prison van with the others being released that day. No more handcuffs. The ride to Gatesville from Harris County seemed so long ago, yet my total time behind bars was just five months and one week. I'd round it up to six months.

My breathing quickened during the ten-minute bus ride to the Gatesville Greyhound Station. The van stopped, and the driver opened the door. As we lined up to get off the vehicle, the driver said, "Watch your step, and good luck, ladies. Stay out of trouble, I don't want to see any of you again."

When I hit the pavement, I could make out a tall figure in a baseball cap standing across the street. Tom.

# Chapter 34
# Home

My first days home were hugs, kisses, and too much food. Tony and Pete always in my sight. The cobwebs and layer of dust on the furniture didn't bother me, I could sweep! One thing that did bother me was the gerbil cage. It was empty. No one told me that during my incarceration, a section of plastic cage tunnel broke apart and the gerbils escaped. Whether it was into our cat's jaws or not was unknown—or unknown to me.

There were small welcome-home parties with my friends over the next few weeks. I was a guest speaker at a women's group meeting. For a short while, I relished moments of fame and celebration. Tony and Pete did not seem overtly wounded. Tom and I were united.

Over the summer we all went to visit my dad in New York and attend Tom's brother's wedding, the one they postponed for me. The family reunions were what we all needed.

The legal side of my saga officially ended. The Supreme Court refused to hear my appeal. That my case got that far was impressive. To get to the Supreme Court you must make it through lower appeal courts first. Trials are guaranteed but getting heard by appellate court, except for death sentences, is not.

I went back to work at Texas Art Supply, per my parole plan. The intensity of my role as convicted spray painter faded as normalcy kicked in.

The parole board that I reported to was down the block from my house on Bradford Street. It was an unmarked, one-story, wood building that I had not noticed before. I walked to my monthly meeting with my parole officer. She summed me up correctly, no threat to society, and spent most of the time talking to me about her job search. She was tired of the parole board, but the money and security was good. Yes, I could relate, having worked at the post office; many postal employees rationalized that the good pay and pension made holding on to a mundane job worthwhile.

My parole office was thinking about going back to college. I encouraged her. When I discussed what to do with the rest of my life, she did not encourage me to return to college. I don't remember her having any positive input about my future. I was still an ex-con, and that's how she viewed me. Showing up every month at the parole board was a way to keep tabs on me, not rehab my life. My emancipation from prison didn't spring me into action. I had my life back, but didn't know what to do with it.

Tom, on the other hand, was a dedicated Buddhist. He was also desperate to leave Texas. His brother and sister lived in Seattle. We talked about moving our family there to start over.

One early fall day I had a meeting with Joe in a park where I told him that Tom and I were seriously thinking about moving with the kids to the West Coast. We thought it would be a fresh start for all of us. He listened without comment. The idea that moving would fundamentally change the relationship he had as a father was one I hadn't given much thought to. He was still in the RCP, so I imagined the move wouldn't affect him that much. His speechless reaction brought it home. Joe was not one to reserve his opinion. I could only assume that he was in shock.

Our politics differed. Our marriage was over. Our children would bond us forever. It would break his heart to be that far from the kids. The allegiance to a cause did not take away his connection to our children. Tony and Pete would miss him, too, and his wife, their stepmother. Moving to Seattle wasn't going to be an easy escape. I was having doubts.

Winter rolled by, and I knew I should be thinking about work beyond Texas Art Supply, as comfortable as it was. Instead of dreaming about my future, it seemed beyond my abilities to do more than make it day to day. I was in the same holding pattern as I was before going to jail. I could get no traction in life.

The next spring, one year after I returned home, Tom went to a Buddhist retreat in the northeast. While he was there, the head honcho died, and Tom extended his stay at this crucial time in the Buddhist community until early summer. He never returned.

My world collapsed. School was out, and Joe took the kids to stay with my dad in New York while I went through a period of going crazy. There is truth to the saying that if you hit bottom, there is no way to go but up. In the end necessity trumped trauma. Tom was gone. I had to take charge of myself and Tony and Pete.

That summer I applied and got into an occupational therapy assistant program at Houston Community College. In the fall I became a full-time student, with my dad's financial help. I did my homework while watching Tony and Pete at YMCA basketball practices four nights a week.

Eventually I remarried, that would be Fred. My kids had yet another stepfather. We moved to a neighborhood where Tony and Pete had access to better schools. At forty-one I finished college. I commuted to the UT medical branch in Galveston, from our home near the Astrodome, for a BA in occupational therapy. After completing the program, I got my OTR license and a job at the VA hospital.

Having a criminal record, I don't know why I assumed I could get a professional license or a job. Maybe the old idealistic naivety doesn't go away. In fact, when I went before the OT licensing board and VA human resources to explain my felony conviction, the people I spoke to were incredulous that I had gone to prison for spray painting. Maybe I was given a break because I didn't fit the stereotype. They treated me like an older, middle-class, white woman looking to start a new career, not an ex-con. I wasn't ever asked, nor did I reveal, what the graffiti had said.

Working for the VA would never have crossed my mind if I hadn't been assigned to do part of my OT internship there and encouraged by my supervisor to apply for a job. When I first got there, I was nervous. I was concerned that all the red, white, and blue would again have me feeling out of place. I wasn't a communist, but hardly a flag waver.

It wasn't the case. I felt right at home. The loss of control, too often experienced in the hospital, and the collective experience of the military resonated with me. The majority of VA patients are low-income and very diverse. The World War II vets all reminded me of my dad. When they told me about their experiences in the Pacific or the Western Front, I told them my father had been in the

21st Infantry and had landed on the beach at Normandy after D-Day. They were impressed, and I felt proud.

My dad, like most of the veterans at the VA, had been drafted and found no pleasure in war. This was especially true of the Vietnam vets I met. Killing for whatever reason was taking a life.

When I told people I worked at the VA, they equated that with patriotism—about my least favorite -*ism*. It isn't about being Un-American, I prefer to think of myself as a global citizen. When I spoke about working with vets, I'd explain that being a military veteran was a big part but not all of who they were. They were people from various backgrounds who each had his own story to tell. Listening was the best part of my job.

I also got interested in gardening. While Fred took pride and care in the flowers and lawn of the house we bought together when we got married, I planted vegetables and fruit trees, sugar snap peas, cucumbers and tomatoes, Meyer lemons, satsuma and figs. I volunteered with community gardeners and saw the connection of healing and harvesting. I kept a hand in a variety of craft arts and physical activities, and followed the home-team Houston Rockets.

In January 2012, two months after I retired from the VA, I went up to the crawl space in the second story of my house. There were three boxes from my Bradford Street home that I had brought to our new house when Fred and I got married in 1989. One box contained all the letters I had sent home, which Tom had saved. Two boxes contained all the letters to Betty Sullivan from jail and prison. Letters from Kelly, Beth, Jack, Wendy, Josie, and Kent. There were a few written by my children. There were letters from Texas Art Supply and Whole Foods coworkers and Tom's Buddhist friends. Many letters were signed by names I didn't remember at all. There were letters from all of Tom's family and my family, some of whom were no longer alive. A huge number of letters were from Tom and the most were from my dad. Daily letters from my dad. In 2005 he had moved in with me and Fred and spent the last six months of his life with us. I was honored to give back to my father.

As I opened and read letter after letter, I cried, because of how awful it all was and how much I didn't remember. The more I read, the more I was filled with gratitude for the flood of encouragement and love. That made me cry too. The letters between Tom and me made me appreciate that he had been there for me and the kids when we needed him most.

So many of the letters sent to me were like diaries, or confessionals, that I felt like a voyeur. I wanted to return them, so the authors would have their personal written records from that time period, but only after I was done. Done with what? Maybe I would put the letters together as a legacy for my kids, let them know the story of their mother. I didn't want my life as a radical and a communist to come off as a regret or mistake, but I knew that I had regrets and had made mistakes. I wanted it all figured out. I wanted to have a new and improved worldview that would be a closure of sorts. That wouldn't happen.

What I did find out through writing is this: I'm more interested in the means than the end. I'm more interested in seeing what people have in common than their differences. I'm not impressed by people or systems that claim to know all the answers or have one answer for all questions. I don't want to lose my passion for social justice, but I don't want that passion to overrule being open to different ideas or changing my mind. I believe that loving my family, loving individuals, is not in competition with any so-called loftier goal or cause. I'd rather feel empathy than anger. I am content to believe there is a basic humanity that everyone shares. That it keeps us connected. That it will save us all.

\* \* \*

More than anything I think, believe, or feel—more than absolutely anything—I want Tony and Pete to know that I love them. Have always loved them. Will always love them. And they are the champions of the world.

# Acknowledgments

I never in my life imagined writing a memoir. My only writing experience was prison letters and OT progress notes. The fact that I finished a book still amazes me. It was the one of the most difficult and necessary things I've undertaken. In the process, I learned that we are all more capable than we perceive, and with the support and kindness of friends, teachers and family, many unimaginable things are possible. My gratitude to those people is boundless.

Thank you Susan Briggs Wright, my first memoir writing class teacher at the Women's Institute in Houston. She gave me positive feedback when I could barely write a sentence. Thank you Lacy Johnson and Leah Lax, my teachers at the two memoir writing classes I took at Inprint. Both of them exposed me to a world of writing craft in a way I could make sense of. Thank you to the teachers at the Bold Face Writing conference at University of Houston who validated my narrative and the aspiration to write it.

Thank you to Andrea Keist, Inder Sandhu and the members of the Meetup critique group they started following an Inprint class. Thank you to the Women in Transition critique group. In the company of peers, I appreciated how many everyday people write so well and how important it is for people to tell their stories.

Thank you Dickson Lam for coaching and tutoring sessions. Thank you Matthew Salesses for content and copyediting and your workshops at Writespace. They made it possible for me to finish this memoir and feel it was worth publishing. All of my wonderful teachers guided me without judgment, gave me encouragement, taught me craft and gave me the courage to forge ahead on this profound journey.

Erin Eriksen, I thank you for your professional insight in collecting and digitizing the images throughout this book and your excitement about my project.

I am indebted to my friends; Lynn Braff (still best friends for over fifty years), Jana Rosenbaum, Leigh Oberholzer, Thelma Zirkelbach and Beth Baker, who read some or all of my drafts and kept me sane. My friend and next door neighbor Linda Kleinworth did all that and my bio picture. To Marilyn Trail, I owe a special thanks for the hours she spent rallying me throughout this four-year-process and inspiring me with her writing skills and perseverance with her own memoir.

Huge thank yous to Jack Livingston, Beth Secor, Wendy Riss and Barbara Burman for responding to this voice from the past and revisiting those days. Thank you for believing in me then and now. Thank you Glen Van Slyke for assisting me with court documents, rehashing the trial and answering every neurotic email. Thank you Tom for reconnecting with me, thoroughly going over all my questions about "what really happened," helping me fill in so many gaps and cheering me on in this process at the risk of coming off as a bad guy.

Thank you to my husband Fred for staying at my side through memories he was not a part of. Thank you to my brother John for his praise and feedback on my last draft. Thank you to my dear cousin Robin for staying alive.

I am so fortunate and grateful to have the love and support of my sons Tony and Pete. A love I still feel undeserving of despite their pleas that they embrace rather than resent their unconventional upbringing. I am fortunate to have a daughter in law, Jennifer, Tony's wife, and their daughter, my granddaughter Joanna Ruth, who is the light of my life.

CPSIA information can be obtained
at www.ICGtesting.com
Printed in the USA
LVOW10s1746071216

516245LV00012B/1601/P